"Sometimes when you send
out letters, you get back
letters. Sometimes you don't.
That's for sure!"

—Lazlo Toth

CITIZEN LAZLO!

The continuing,
unrelenting correspondence
of Lazlo Toth, American!

by Don Novello

Workman Publishing, New York

Photo Credits.
Front cover. Right center: Rudi Frey, *Time*
Magazine. All other photos: AP/Wide World
Photos. Back Cover (clockwise). Nixon
Presidential Materials Project, National
Archives; AP/Wide World Photos (3); Richard
Nixon Library & Birth Place; John Marriott.

Library of Congress Cataloging-in-Publication Data

Novello, Don.
Citizen Lazlo! : the Lazlo letters, volume 2 / by Don
Novello.
p.   cm.
ISBN 1-56305-182-6 (pbk.) : $7.95
1. United States—Politics and government—1981–
1989—Humor. 2. United States—Politics and government—1989—Humor. 3. United States—Social
life and customs—1971—Humor. 4. Novello, Don-
Correspondence. I. Title.
E876.N68   1992
973'.0207—dc20

Workman Publishing Company
708 Broadway
New York, New York 10003

Manufactured in the United States of America
First printing May 1992
1   3   5   7   9   10   8   6   4   2

CITIZEN LAZLO!
The Lazlo Letters
Volume 2

2282 N. Beachwood
Los Angeles, California
March 31, 1977

Former President Gerald Ford
Desert White House (Casa Desert)
Thunderbird Golf Course Estates
Palm Springs, California

NO IMITATIONS

White House Will Roll Out Real Eggs

WASHINGTON (AP)—With Jimmy Carter, youngsters will get real eggs, not the plastic imitations used on the White House lawn during the last two Easter egg rolls.

Dear President Ford,

Do you get what they're trying to say? I think they want to make your administration look "plastic". Well, I think the joke is on them because all you have to do is read one paragraph more and it says about four dozen eggs are being provided by the Georgia Egg Commission. Get it? It's all politics! Carter's from Georgia, remember? I wish he was from Washington, that way he could walk to the corner and get the eggs. Is sending to Georgia for four dozen eggs going to help fight inflation like you were trying to do? You were doing something - not just symbolism! If just symbolism is so great, why can't they just ride around the block to symbolize a drive to Georgia and buy the eggs at the corner grocery store to symbolize common sense like most normal Presidents have!

You cut out using real eggs, the paper said, because people would squish them all over the White House lawn. That was a good reason - but how about cholesterol? You want to see the egg industry run for cover, just mention the word "cholesterol". They're running scared (latest reports make eggs sound about as good for you as Draino) and they probably figure they need this Easter exposure to keep in the ball game with Kelloggs. And I understand the sales of Egg McMuffins is down, too.

And then (same section of the paper), I saw the topper. All during the campaign he kept talking about cutting the number of people in government, and even in his fireside-cardigan speech he said he was going to cut the White House staff by one third, and now it comes out that his staff is larger than yours! They say it's because he's getting so many letters, he needs all those extra people to help him answer the mail. I don't know who's writing to him - not me!

WHAT THIS COUNTRY NEEDS, THIS COUNTRY HAD!
JERRY FORD WASN'T SO BAD!

Lazlo Toth

Lazlo Toth

Gerald R. Ford

Mr. Lazlo Toth
2282 North Beachwood
Los Angeles, California
90068

Betty and I are deeply grateful for your thoughtful
message. We treasure the friendship of our fellow Americans,
and our hearts are warmed by your kind words and good wishes.

Jerry Ford

WELK TENANTS FUMING, NOT BUBBLING, OVER RENT HIKE

Mr. Lawrence Welk
c/o Lawrence Welk Mobile Home Park
Escondido, California

Dear Mr. Welk,

I've always liked your fine selection of
tunes and people and know you wouldn't run
a Mobile Home Park any different! I could
puke! I just read an article in the paper
headlined <u>TROUBLE IN BUBBLELAND</u>. One guy
is saying the sewage backs up and fills his
bathtub, somebody else is saying you can't water your lawn
and take a shower at the same time. Too bad! Who ever
heard of watering your lawn and taking a shower at the same
time - that's crazy. I drew this for you so you could put
it in the Mobile Home Park newspaper. Maybe it will help
shut up all those malcontents.

The press did the same thing to Earl Butz and
President Nixon that they're trying to do to you.
Stonewall! Don't tell them anything. It's
enough to make me want to move to Alaska. Only
one problem - Snow tires!

You wouldn't want to put them on before you left - you'd wear
down all your treads! But if you take them with you, where do
you put them? Not in the trunk - you need the trunk for the
luggage! If you tied one on the hood it wouldn't be practical -
I like to check my levels everyday and it's too much of a bur-
don taking that tire on and off so often. Plus the fact that
you still have to find somewhere else to put the other three!
I guess I'm staying. So, even though you were forced to increase
some rents by 42%, how much would it cost me for a reasonable
size lot?

Keep up the beat!

Lazlo Toth

LAZLO TOTH / 2282 N. Beachwood / Los Angeles, California / 90068

9

2282 N. Beachwood
Los Angeles, California
March 28, 1977
90068 - ZIP CODE

Hon. Edward R. Roybal
House of Representatives
Washington, D.C.

Dear Mr. Congressman,

First of all I want to congradulate you on getting
that terrific pay raise ($12,900!) and balancing it
by passing the rigorous new ethics code.
As I understand it now, you're up to $57,500 per
year but you can't have any more slush funds and
you have to limit your outside income to 15% of
your salary ($8,625 more).

Well, I for one think you deserve every dollar of
it! Most congressman types could be making BIG
bucks in private industry and we wouldn't want you
all quitting and going with Motorola or somebody
like that. And afterall, how can you set examples
for regular Americans if you're underpaid, too!

Today in the barber shop (Ned's), a new barber who's
only been there for less than a year started sprout-
ing off about one of our former Presidents and I put
him in his place fast. But, he also started in about
Congress (you), and he said that even though your
new raise starts immediately, the rigorous new ethics
code doesn't start for two years. That sure doesn't
sound right to me, but I told him I'd check on it.
Who's right?

                    Together we can beat this inflation!

                         Lazlo Toth

                    Lazlo Toth

EDWARD R. ROYBAL
25TH DISTRICT, CALIFORNIA

2404 RAYBURN OFFICE BUILDING
WASHINGTON, D.C. 20515
———
LOS ANGELES OFFICE:
ROOM 7106, NEW FEDERAL P.O. BLDG.
300 N. LOS ANGELES STREET
LOS ANGELES, CALIFORNIA 90012
PHONE: 688-4870

Congress of the United States
House of Representatives
Washington, D.C. 20515

COMMITTEE ON
APPROPRIATIONS

SUBCOMMITTEES:
LABOR-HEALTH EDUCATION AND
WELFARE
TREASURY-POSTAL SERVICE-GENERAL
GOVERNMENT
LEGISLATIVE

SELECT COMMITTEE ON AGING
CHAIRMAN-SUBCOMMITTEE ON
HOUSING AND CONSUMER INTERESTS
DEMOCRATIC CAUCUS COMMITTEE
ON ORGANIZATION, STUDY AND
REVIEW

April 15, 1977

Mr. Lazlo Toth
2282 N. Beachwood
Los Angeles, California 90068

Dear Mr. Toth:

Thank you for your recent letter in which you expressed support
of the congressional pay raise, but questioned the fact that
the new ethics code would not take effect immediately.

For your information, I am enclosing a summary of the rules
changes with the respective effective dates. As you know, not
all the changes are effective immediately. Only one of the
changes will not take effect until 1979 and this pertains to
outside earned income. Clearly, this is one of the major changes
in the code of ethics and I appreciate being given this opportunity
to explain why this effective date is so much later than the
others.

In drawing up the new code, those charged with this responsibility
felt that to make this rule effective immediately might well create
an ex post facto situation. Since Members of Congress were elected
to Congress without any knowledge that such a limit would be placed
on their income, it was decided that the fairest way to handle the
situation would be to have the rule change apply to all succeeding
Congresses. In this way Members of Congress would be given the
opportunity to wind down from current commitments or activities.

Thank you for your interest.

With best wishes.

Sincerely,

Edward R. Roybal

EDWARD R. ROYBAL
Member of Congress

ERR:as
Enclosure

April 25, 1977

President
Kellogg's Company
Battlecreek, Michigan

Dear Sir:

Good morning! I just finished eating some of your
cereal (Sugar Pops), and thought I'd write while I
was thinking of you.
I know you're probably extra busy because of the
drought, but I feel what concerns me may be important
to many other Americans as well, and I feel you should
be aware of my problem.

Regarding the Kellogg's Rice Krispies Rice to Riches
Contest: On the back of the Kellogg's Rice Krispies
box it says there are three categories for recipes
using Rice Krispies - 1. Best Main Dish Recipe - $10,000
                       2. Best Dessert Recipe - $10,000
                       3. Best Snack Recipe - $10,000

My recipe - Oysters Califano - doesn't fit into any of
the categories! I asked the checkout girl what she thought
I should do and she said to put it under "Main Dish", but
I told her it wasn't a main dish, but everybody is so darn
busy they just don't listen! If you served this as a main
dish, everybody would be waiting for more to eat after they
ate it, and you would get a lot of letters complaining and
it wouldn't do me any good to say I did it because the
checkout girl said to do it like that! And besides, she'd
probably want half the money ($5,000) for suggesting the
category! Nuts to that! So, I thought I'd write directly
to you for the proper answer. I know you might have to
create a whole new category for this -
                       4. Best Appetizer Recipe - $10,000
but I think it would be the right thing to do. Let me know,
I've got the box top and recipe ready to go!

                    Standing by for a category,

                    Lazlo Toth

                    Lazlo Toth

P.S. I like the Variety Pack best, but I don't think you
      should keep putting in the Sugar Pops. I notice it's
      always the last one left and half the time I feel like
      throwing it away. And all my friends feel the same!
      Why not replace it with Rice Krispies or Corn Flakes?

May 11, 1977

Mr. Lazlo Toth
2282 N Beachwood
Los Angeles, CA 90068

Our File 051177F551

Dear Mr. Toth:

Thank you for writing to Kellogg Company about our Rice-to-Riches
Contest. I'm happy you are entering this contest.

The decision about the category for your recipe must be made by you.
I can't tell you how to classify your recipe. You will have to do
this yourself. Although your idea for having a "best appetizer"
category is not new to us, we appreciate your interest.

With regard to your statement about taking KELLOGG'S SUGAR CORN POPS
out of the VARIETY ASSORTMENT, I must tell you it isn't there now!
SUGAR CORN POPS is found in KELLOGG'S JUMBO ASSORTMENT. Enclosed is
a list showing the different assortment packs we market.

Good luck in the contest.

Sincerely,

Ms. Monti Trent-Zinn
Consumer Consultant

MTZ/ja

cc President
    Helen Olsen & Company

KELLOGG'S JUMBO (18 pkgs)

3 KELLOGG'S CORN FLAKES
2 KELLOGG'S RICE KRISPIES
2 KELLOGG'S SUGAR FROSTED FLAKES
1 KELLOGG'S SUGAR POPS
2 KELLOGG'S RAISIN BRAN
2 KELLOGG'S SUGAR SMACKS
2 KELLOGG'S SPECIAL K
1 KELLOGG'S PRODUCT 19
1 KELLOGG'S APPLE JACKS
1 KELLOGG'S FROOT LOOPS
1 KELLOGG'S FROSTED RICE

KELLOGG'S VARIETY (10 pkgs)

2 KELLOGG'S CORN FLAKES
1 KELLOGG'S RICE KRISPIES
2 KELLOGG'S RAISIN BRAN
1 KELLOGG'S SUGAR FROSTED FLAKES
1 KELLOGG'S SPECIAL K
1 KELLOGG'S PRODUCT 19
1 KELLOGG'S 40Z BRAN FLAKES
1 KELLOGG'S FROOT LOOPS

2282 N. Beachwood
Los Angeles, California
April 25, 1977
90068 - ZIP CODE

Hon. Edward R. Roybal
House of Representatives
Washington, D.C.

Dear Congressman Roybal,

I know that it's cherry blossom time and all, and want
you to know I really appreciate your taking the time to
answer my question pertaining to the congressional pay
raise and the rigorous new ethics code.

As I understand your answer, the reason the ethics code
doesn't take effect for two years is because members of
Congress were elected to Congress without any knowledge
that a limit would be placed on their income - and so
it was decided that the fairest way to handle the situation would be to have the rule change apply to all succeeding Congresses.
My new question is: Since members of Congress were elected to Congress without any knowledge that they would
be getting more income (salary raise), wouldn't the fairest way to handle that situation be to have the salary
raise apply to all succeeding Congresses, too?

Your pay was raised because your outside income was cur-
tailed. The two were tied together! If one is postponed,
shouldn't the other one be too?

                    With best wishes.

                    Sincerely,

                    Laslo Toth

                    Lazlo Toth

EDWARD R. ROYBAL
25TH DISTRICT, CALIFORNIA

2404 RAYBURN OFFICE BUILDING
WASHINGTON, D.C. 20515

LOS ANGELES OFFICE:
ROOM 7106, NEW FEDERAL P.O. BLDG.
300 N. LOS ANGELES STREET
LOS ANGELES, CALIFORNIA 90012
PHONE: 688-4870

Congress of the United States
House of Representatives
Washington, D.C. 20515

April 29, 1977

COMMITTEE ON
APPROPRIATIONS

SUBCOMMITTEES:
LABOR-HEALTH EDUCATION AND
WELFARE
TREASURY-POSTAL SERVICE-GENERAL
GOVERNMENT
LEGISLATIVE

SELECT COMMITTEE ON AGING
CHAIRMAN-SUBCOMMITTEE ON
HOUSING AND CONSUMER INTERESTS
DEMOCRATIC CAUCUS COMMITTEE
ON ORGANIZATION, STUDY AND
REVIEW

Mr. Lazlo Toth
2282 N. Beachwood
Los Angeles, California 90068

Dear Mr. Toth:

Again, I wish to thank you for your interest in the
Congressional pay raise and the new ethics code.

You will be interested to know that there is a strong feeling
among Members of Congress to postpone the pay raise until
the 96th Congress. Approximately 100 Members have already
joined in cosponsoring the Congressional Pay Raise Deferral
Act, H.R. 1365. In addition, during consideration of the
First Concurrent Resolution on the Budget for Fiscal Year
1978, the House voted to reduce the budget authority so that it
would not reflect the recent congressional pay raise.

While the Budget Resolution itself did not pass, I have been
informed that the revised resolution will reflect the House's
wish to delete monies for the pay raise. Should the new budget
resolution be approved, further legislation would be required
to actually delete the salary increase.

With best wishes.

Sincerely,

EDWARD R. ROYBAL
Member of Congress

ERR:as

15

NO REPLY !

Penn State De-Sexes Its Alma Mater

UNIVERSITY PARK, Pa. (AP)—
Penn State University has a new,
"nonsexist" version of its 75-year-old
alma mater.

2282 N. Beachwoo[d]
Los Angeles, Cal[if.]
May 2, 1977

Dr. John W. Oswald
President, Penn State University
Penn State University
University Park, Pa.

Dear Doctor Oswald,

I just read where Penn State went and "de-sexed" its
Alma Mater and you now have a "non sexist version of
the 75-year-old song". The article said you did it because your school now is co-ed and the women students
never "stood at boyhood's gate" and at no time were
"molded into men" like the song says.
Boyhood's Gate - where's that, somewhere near Trenton?
There is no Boyhood's Gate - that's just symbolism!
It doesn't even exist! And since it doesn't exist, why
not let everybody stand there? It's not costing you
anything! I would think the women would find it "sexist" <u>not</u> to be able to stand at Boyhood's Gate! Anyway,
I read that you changed it to "Childhood's Gate". As
a songwriter (for President Nixon among others), I feel
obliged to offer some suggestions. Changing the lyrics
of songs is my specialty and I am offering my time FREE
because you are an educational institution.

I read that <u>"Thou didst mold us, dear old State,</u>
            <u>into men, into men"</u> was changed to:
        <u>"Thou didst mold us, dear old State,</u>
            <u>dear old State, dear old State."</u>
You just can't drop half a thought and then try to get
away with it by repeating the last phrase! I know that's
an old college trick but the days of taking short cuts
are over! You went and changed the whole meaning of the
song and instead of "de-sexing" it, you went and ruined
it! All it says now is "you molded us, dear old State".
Molded us (you) into what? Did it mold you into molds?
I think that's what it's saying, and I don't think that's
what people want out of college!
If you want to go changing something, why don't you change
the "Thou didst's"! You kept the worst part! Nobody says
"Thou didst" anymore! That's the trouble if you hang around
a college town too long, you loose perspective! Watch television, that's almost as good as traveling, plus it's a
lot less expensive. Electricity is less than gas and that's
just the starters. Then come the Motels, tolls, etc.
I suggest you change the "Thou didst" to "You did". Once
you get out of Amish country, "you did" is about all you're
going to hear. Let me know if I'm wrong.

                    I amst,

                    Lazlo Toth

                    Lazlo Toth

2282 N. Beachwood
Los Angeles, California
May 6, 1977

President Richard M. Nixon (Roland)
La Casa Pacifica
Republic of San Clemente
San Clemente, California

Dear President Nixon,

Boy, did you put David Frost in his place! And to think you made
a million dollars besides - Congradulations!
My favorite part was when you started talking about the tulips
in the fields around Camp David. It was like poetry! Did you
get that from Tony Orlando? It reminded me of a speech he
gave right before he sang <u>My Way</u>, on his farewell show.
And I also liked the part when it looked like Frost had you
pinned in the corner and you took a few seconds to think the
situation over, and then said, "I'm sorry, but I can't inter-
pret that at this time". Perfect! Frost just sat there looking like a plant that needs watering. He didn't know <u>what</u> to
say! And the next thing, the Weed Eater commercial was on, and
when the interview came back on he asked a <u>new</u> question!

<u>One question</u>: Did Frost pick the home where you taped the in-
terviews? I missed half the darn thing because of all the planes.
Every time a plane went over I thought it was going over <u>my</u>
place, and I'd get up and look. Later, I found out from my
friend (George Tuttle) that he heard the planes, too, so we figured since we live pretty far from one another and since neither
of us saw any planes, it must have been on the tape. You couldn't
tell from watching you - you just sat there real calm and didn't
even mention the planes! You sure are some actor! Move over,
Broderick Crawford!

<u>One complaint</u>: I don't like you talking about your public life
being through - deep six that idea! We need you!

<u>One suggestion</u>: How about running for Governor of California?
And since President Ford is living in California, too (Palm Springs),
how about trying to talk him into running for Lt. Governor? I
hope all of a sudden he doesn't think he's too good for number two.
I can see the billboards now - THE PRESIDENTS FOR GOVERNOR AND LT.
GOVERNOR! What clout! What experience! California couldn't say
no! It would be a great base for you to start your campaign to be
Ambassador to China! Carter would have to appoint you after you
were <u>elected</u> again! And in the meantime, California could truly
turn into the Free Enterprise Shangraila it was meant to be!

Like you say, "I was not a good butcher". California doesn't need
a good butcher for Governor - we need a SENSITIVE leader! Afterall,
you're not running for Governor of the A&P! Let's go! Next stop,
Sacramento!

                    One of over 50 million loyal boosters,

                              Lazlo Toth

          Lazlo Toth

LAZLO TOTH
2282 North Beachwood
Los Angeles, Calif. 90068

August, 1977

TO: President Jimmy Carter

FROM: Lazlo Toth

RE: THE GALVESTON CANAL (The answer to many of our problems)

The main reason we're having all this trouble today with the
Panamanians is because of the name. We should have called it
The American Canal instead of The Panama Canal - no wonder
they think they own it!
The Panama Canal problem is not going to go away, and the
only solution is an American Canal! Built by Americans!
Run by Americans! On American soil! With restaurants near
by with American food!
And besides being a truly American Canal, it can solve a lot
of other problems, too.

- Illegal aliens can't get across
  The canal will put a big swim between us and Mexico and
  help keep illegal aliens down where they're legal.

- No more unemployment
  They'll be work for everybody on the canal! It's
  going to be a big job.

PUSH→ THE GALVESTON CANAL

- Middle East Problem Solved
  The 1,525 mile long, ½ mile wide, island of
  land can be pushed out to sea (Golf of Mexico),
  and serve as a homeland for the Palestinians.
  Besides being a wonderful place for car races,
  it will put a nice buffer of Galvestinians between us and the Cubans.

- Helps Reduce Some Air Fares
  Air fares between New Orleans and San diego
  will cost only $30 round trip (shuttle) - a
  savings of $240 at present distances!

Lazlo Toth

18

THE WHITE HOUSE

WASHINGTON

December 22, 1977

Dear Mr. Toth:

Thank you for your suggestions for President
Carter's government reorganization project.

Study teams within the President's Reorganization Project have begun examining
areas of federal government activity. In
coming months these project teams will be
developing possible improvements in
government organization.

Let me assure you that your suggestions
will be brought to the attention of the
appropriate team.

Sincerely,

Richard A. Pettigrew
Assistant to the President
for Reorganization

Mr. Lazlo Toth
2282 North Beachwood
Los Angeles, California   90068

```
                          2282 N. Beachwood
                          Los Angeles, California
                          90068 - ZIP CODE U.S.A.
                          November 3, 1977
```

His Royal Highness Prince Charles
c/o Her Royal Highness Queen Elizabeth
Balmoral Castle
London, England (GB)

Dear Prince of the Blood Royal,

On behalf of all the American people I would like to say,
"Thank you for a splendid visit, 'ol chap!" I saw you on
T.V. (television) and you are looking good! You look 100%
better with your hair short! Everybody does!

I asked your Mother for a photo when she was here for the
Bycentenial, but she said she only gives it out to people
she knows "personally". I've gotten photos from Sammy
Davis Jr., Mayor Rizzo, etc., and you must realize that
it's things like that that gives royalty a bad name! Does
she think she's better than everybody else just cause she's
the Queen? What if Mayor Rizzo did that? Just turn the chairs
around a little and you can see that I've got a good point!

I hope you are not like your Mother and that you will send
me your picture. The way I figure it, someday you will be
the King of England! Your Mother is the Queen, you've got
it made! Just keep it up!

Here's a little tune I wrote special for your visit to
America. It's called PRINCE CHARLES' VISIT TO AMERICA.
(To the tune of 'Ol McDonald / Moon River.)

                 Prince Charles' visit to America
                 was brief, yes!, but it was polite.
                 A regular fellow touring treatment plants
                 eeeee-aiiiiii-eeeeee-aiiiiii-o,
                 my huckleberry friend.
                 Even though some people thought
                 he was too polite -
                 NOBODY said he wasn't dull.
                 Waiting round the bend.
                 Prince Charles' visit to America
                 Let's do it again sometime!
                 Prince Charles' visit to America
                 Let's do it again sometime!

          Keep sending your old boats to Long Beach!

                         Lazlo Toth
                         Lazlo Toth
```
```

BUCKINGHAM PALACE

From: M. M. Colborne, Esq.   29th November, 1977

Dear Mr. Toth,

    I have been instructed to write and thank
you for your letter of 3rd November to The Prince
of Wales.

    Unfortunately, His Royal Highness is unable
to send you a photograph. It is a general policy
that Members of The Royal Family only give photographs to associations with which they are connec-
ted or personal friends.

    Thank you for writing.

Yours sincerely,

(miss) Jane Oakley

for Secretary

Mr. L. Toth

2282 N. Beachwood
Los Angeles, California
U.S.A.- 90068- ZIP CODE
November 19, 1977

Commanding Officer
AIR CANADA
Place Ville Marie (Marie's Town Place)
Montreale 113, Quebec

Dear Sir:

I recently flew on your airline and I must say I was more than
somewhat disappointed!

First of all, the stewardess asked me if I wanted to see the
movie. I said, "No, thank you". Later, when I asked for some
ear phones, she said, "I thought you didn't want the movie?"
She thought right, I didn't want the movie, I just wanted to
listen to some music, I told her.
She said the music was only for people who paid for the movie!
"Otherwise, how would we know you weren't listening to the movie,"
she said. How about the honor system? In my country they don't
go around accusing paying customers of cheating! If I could afford
to fly to Canada, do you think I couldn't afford $2.50 for a lousy
movie? Besides, that's $2.50 in Canadian dollars - cheaper still!
I saw a lot of people watching the movie who didn't pay for it!
Why don't you charge to watch the movie instead of to listen to
it? Why can you watch a movie for nothing but have to pay to listen to some records? It's just not fair! Next thing you know,
you'll probably be charging people to look at record albums!

Also, my tomatoe soup was ice cold! I thought it was because I
was the only one polite enough to wait until everybody got served
before I started eating, but when I told the stewardess my soup
was cold, she said it wasn't tomatoe soup, that it was tomatoe
juice! How was I suppose to know it was tomatoe juice? What was
the soup spoon there for then? I wasted two or three minutes eating it like that! Why don't you label those things? If you can
lable "Salad dressing", why not juice and soup? I knew the salad
dressing was salad dressing - what else could it have been - jello?
Come on! Why do you label something that doesn't need a label and
not label the thing I mistook for something else?

I think that by labeling the soup and the juice and starting free
music you can make a giant step towards better understandings between both of our countries. Things are unstable enough without
these things getting in the way, too.

                          your neighbor (votre neibor),

                          Lazlo Toth
                          Lazlo Toth

AIR CANADA  PLACE VILLE MARIE, MONTRÉAL, CANADA   H3B 3P7

OFFICE OF THE PRESIDENT
BUREAU DU PRÉSIDENT

December 29, 1977

Mr. Lazlo Toth
2282 North Beachwood
Los Angeles, California 90068
U.S.A.

Dear Mr. Toth:

We were very sorry to learn of your disappointment in some aspects of our service during your travel with us in November, but appreciate your giving us your observations.

Recorded music is available on some of our flights at no charge; however, on flights where music is provided in conjunction with a movie, it is felt that, in fairness to all passengers, the charge for the movie must be levied on all passengers making use of the earphones.

Soup is very seldom served by the airlines, because of the difficulties inherent in its provision, and it is regretted that this was not clarified with you.

Thank you for your interest in writing.

Yours very truly,

A.R. Godbold
Manager, Customer Relations

2282 N. Beachwood
Los Angeles, California
90068 - ZIP CODE
November 21, 1977

San Clemente Chamber of Commerce
San Clemente, California
92672 - ZIP CODE

Dear Gentlemen,

Thank you! Thank you! Thank you! I think it's wonderful
that you're going to let people tour La Casa Pacifica (The
Pacific House) so people can see for themselves how our
President spends his time. A thrill? Yes!

Most unfortunately, I've been out of the country on a private foreign mission, and I missed the announcement that you
were selling tickets. I just hope it isn't too late! I've
been an admirer of President Nixon's since way back! I'd
stick with him through anything! And I have!

Please send two tickets - I'll be bringing a friend! Also,
I would like to have tickets for <u>front seats</u>, if it's possible. I like to be as close as possible to the driver - I
find you can always pick up extra info if you're near the
center of the action. It's worked out for me!

                    Thank you a million!
                    This is my dream!
                    Don't forget the <u>front</u> seats!

                    Lazlo Toth

                    Lazlo Toth

encl: $5 American for two seats to La Casa Pacifica

SAN CLEMENTE CHAMBER OF COMMERCE
BOX 338 - SAN CLEMENTE - CALIFORNIA 92672

Lazlo Toth
2282 North Beachwood
Los Angeles, CA   90068

Thank you for being interested in the 50th Birthday of the
City of San Clemente.

We are sorry the President Nixon Tour is sold out.

Sincerely,

The San Clemente Chamber of Commerce

Sorry!

Enclosed $5.00 CASH

His Imperial Majesty
Mohammad Reza Pahlavi
Aryamehr
Shahanahah of Iran
Tehran, Iran (Persia)

2282 N. Beachwood
Los Angeles, California
U.S.A. 90068 - ZIP CODE
November 23, 1977

Dear Your Shah,

I think it's a shame, your Shah, the way certain people were acting during your recent visit to the U.S. I would apologize if they were Americans, but I understand they were all yours! I can always spot an Iranian student in this country - he's the one with a bag over his head! (You can use that!) I thought it was probably an old Persian custom, then I heard the reason is because SAVAK secret police might spot them and then they would be in hot sauce back home. But that doesn't justify them throwing tear gas at you! They're probably the same ones that are saying all _your_ supporters were _paid_ to come. They're all just jealous! Everybody can't get to be Shah!

Sometimes I think all the malcontents in the world are financed by the same people - otherwise, how could they all have the same complaints? Maybe you can have somebody check into that!

It says in the paper that Iran and the U.S. have a "special relationship". My friend, George Tuttle, says translated from diplomatic jargon that means we own you. Any truth in that? That's a story going around and we might as well get right to the point. Those kind of questions are going to come up if you ever have a free press in your country, so better think it over. The press is nosy!

Please send me your picture!

Lazlo Toth

Lazlo Toth

IMPERIAL EMBASSY OF IRAN

WASHINGTON, D. C.

JANUARY 3, 1978

DEAR MR. TOTH:

I AM PLEASED TO INFORM YOU THAT YOUR RECENT LETTER ADDRESSED TO HIS IMPERIAL MAJESTY, THE SHAHANSHAH ARYAMEHR, HAS RECEIVED HIS MAJESTY'S GRACIOUS ATTENTION. IT HAS NOW BEEN FORWARDED TO US FROM THE IMPERIAL COURT IN TEHRAN WITH THE REQUEST THAT WE THANK YOU FOR YOUR KIND SENTIMENTS.

I AM ALSO ENCLOSING FOR YOU HEREWOTH A PHOTOGRAPH OF HIS MAJESTY, AS YOU REQUESTED.

WITH KIND REGARDS AND VERY BEST WISHES FOR A HAPPY AND PEACEFUL NEW YEAR.

SINCERELY YOURS,

NASSER GHOUSHBEIGUI
COUNSELOR

2282 N. Beachwood
Los Angeles, California
90068 - ZIP CODE
September 4, 1977

Ms. Monti Trent-Zinn
Kelloggs Company
Battle Creek, Michigan
49016 - ZIP CODE

Dear Ms. Monti Trent-Zinn,

After careful deliberation and many near sleepless
nights, I have decided to enter my recipe for Oysters
Califano under <u>MAIN DISH</u>. ($10,000 First Prize)

For a long time I just didn't feel right about making it
a main dish because it just didn't seem like it would
be enough. But then my friend George Tuttle saw on the
box that to be eligible the recipe had to have at least
four cups of Rice Krispies and by adding that extra
amount of Rice Krispies everybody seems more than full.
All of a sudden, it's a <u>MAIN DISH</u>!

I feel pretty confident that I can win the contest.
I've tried it out on different people and they all agree
that it's a MAIN DISH! I had a great Uncle who was the
guy that thought up the idea of putting a cherry on
top of grapefruit. Before that, they used to use little
pieces of banana. But as soon as he came up with the
idea of the cherry, everybody agreed that he was right.
It was a natural! Who would ever think that a cherry
and a grapefruit could be eaten together? The same goes
for oysters and Rice Krispies! You just have to get
used to it.

I see you sent a copy of your letter to Helen Olsen.
Now - where do I send the recipe? I thought maybe I should
send it to you, but then I saw that you sent a carbon
copy of your letter to me to her, so I thought maybe I
should submit the recipe direct to her since she's probably the one who tests them out and has people eat them.
I just hope you don't get people who don't like sea food,
because it wouldn't be fair! Preferably, I would like this
recipe tested in <u>Boston</u>, if it's possible.

Also, I'm sorry I got mixed up about the Sugar Corn Pops
not being in the Variety Pack - I meant to say Jumbo
Assortment. I just made a little mistake - I don't think
it's something to make a big deal about.

Standing by for an address,

Lazlo Toth

Lazlo Toth

2282 N. Beachwood
Los Angeles, Calif
90068 - ZIP CODE
December 20, 1977

President
Kellogg's Company
Battlecreek, Michigan

Dear Mr. President,

Good morning! I know you're busy, but this will only take
a few seconds of your time.

A number of months ago (3) I entered your Kellogg's Rice-
to Riches Contest, MAIN DISH, which has a $10,000 First Prize.
On the back of the package, it says that a winners list is
available if you send a self addressed envelope to the address
given. Almost three months have gone by since the contest
closed, the year is almost over, and I have not been notified
that I won, nor have I received a winners list like you pro-
mised! It said winner's would be notified after October 30,
1977, but it doesn't say how long after October 30th! But most
normal people would think you meant at least this year!

My problem is this - I don't know which year to report the
$10,000 winnings on my income tax. That is, IF I win! I'm
99% positive that I will, but time has a way of stealing away
optimism, and every day that I don't get notified I get a bit
more doubtful. Anyway, it would be better for me to report it
this year ('77), since I'll be selling some puppies early next
year, so I'll have extra income from that for '78. So, if you
could get me the money right away, before the first of the year,
I'd appreciate it. Afterall, I'm not raising dogs for Uncle
Sam! And how about all the other folks that took the time and
effort to send you recipes and self addressed envelopes? Many
are on pins and needles -- what's the problem? You don't seem
to have any trouble getting out the cereal! I see it everywhere!

Also, I would appreciate it very much if you would please not
forward this letter to Ms. Monti Trent-Zinn. The last time I
wrote her, she sent me back a Xerox copy of the box top with a
pentel mark pointing to some information on the box top! Not
even the courtesy to write decent English! We had a little run
in awhile back over taking the Sugar Pops out of the Jumbo pack.
I said "Variety Pack" by mistake, and she jumped all over me
for it! Jumbo pack, Variety pack, what does it all matter in
the end? I say, "Order a large orange juice once in a while, so
what if it's expensive, live it up!" You should tell her that!
Relax! What's the hurry just drawing circles around box tops!
Stop and smell the roses and be nice to people! Afterall, they're
not just people, they're your customers, too! And three months
is long enough!

I'll be eating eggs until I hear from you,

Lazlo Toth

Lazlo Toth

CONSUMER SERVICE DEPARTMENT
235 PORTER STREET ● BATTLE CREEK, MICHIGAN 49016

January 19, 1978

Lazlo Toth
2282 N Beachwood
Los Angeles, CA 90068

Our File B051177F551

Dear Mr. Toth:

How could you have mistaken my actions so completely!? I have a
reputation around here for being very thoughtful and helpful to all of
our consumers, and it was my consideration of the limited time you had
before the entry deadline that gave me the idea of sending just the
panel (not a boxtop) copy with circles drawn on it. By the way, I
didn't use a Pentel for making the circles. It was an Eagle Flash II
or a Flash 30 and a Major Accent 49. I never liked Pentels. Mention
one in a conversation and people think you have a speech impediment.
Why make yourself sound like you have something you don't?

Mr. Toth, you probably did not send in a self-addressed, stamped envelope
or you would have received your Winners' List by now. Nevertheless, I am
making an exception in your case and am enclosing the winners' list for
you. You will notice, I'm sure, that your name is not on the list. I
hope you'll be able to sell lots of dogs in 1978 to make up for the loss
of the $10,000.00 winnings.

No offense, sir, but as a vegetarian I thought your recipe sounded awful.
I'm always leery of people who eat mollusks. It seems to me that people
who would eat a valuable little oyster whose only purpose is to make a
pearl, would probably eat anything they could get their hands on! These
same people more than likely also bake and eat "tuna" casseroles when
everyone knows that most of the "tuna" sold anymore is really dolphin.
Oyster and tuna-eaters are just wiping out the dolphin population of the
world and wrecking our country's economy. When our sweet sand and sea
creatures go, marine research goes; when marine research goes, computers
go; and when the computers go, well, there goes the country. Meat, fish
and fowl-eaters should really stop and think what they're doing, for all
our sakes!

Get back to basics, I say. Grains and vegetables--these are the proper
things to be eating. Raise your vibrations! Be a part of the Peaceable
Kingdom! That's what it's all about! If you had been thinking as a
vegetable person, this whole misunderstanding would have never happened.
You would have realized I spent much effort in your behalf and I did so
graciously. I even said "Good luck in the contest." I didn't have to say
that, but I did. (I try to give encouragement to all our consumers.)

Mr. Toth, I really don't have time to smell a rose because I'm so busy
being helpful and kind to all our consumers (crotchety cooks included).
So, you go smell the rose. When you do, be sure to inhale deeply; the
pollen will do you worlds of good.

Sincerely,

Ms. Monti Trent-Zinn
Consumer Consultant

MTZ/ja

enc winners' list

KELLOGG'S "RICE TO RICHES" RECIPE CONTEST

WINNERS LIST CATEGORY: DESSERTS
TOP WINNER. $10,000.00
ANN TRULOVE. . . . .Farmington, NM 87401

RUNNER-UP: $5,000.00
GWILA A. PEMBERTON. Memphis, Tn. 38112

$100.00 WINNERS
1. Marjorie Blumberg . . Chevy Chase, MD 20015
2. Edna Buckley . . . . .Collins, NY 14034
3. Catherine Bugnitz . . . . .Florissant, MO 63033
4. Barbara J. Callahan . . . . . . .Houston, TX 77009
5. Ruth W. Churchill. . . . .Red Hook, NY 12571
6. Marilyn Colatrella . . . .

WINNER LIST CATEGORY: MAIN DISH
TOP WINNER — $10,000.00
JACQUELYN J. TAMARGO — Canton, Oh. 44708

RUNNER-UP — $5,000.00
MABEL HAUGEN . . . . Beloit, Wi. 53511

$100.00 WINNERS
1. Maxine B. Archibald . . . . .Largo, Fl. 33540
2. Mrs. C.M. Arkinson . . Orangeburg, SC 29115
3. Anita Atoulikian . . . . . .Parma Oh 44129
4. Aline Ballentine . . . . .Ellenville, NY 12428
5. Catherine A. Becker . . . .

WINNERS LIST CATEGORY: SNACKS
TOP WINNER: $10,000.00
LAUREL POLANICK. San Francisco, CA 94

RUNNER-UP: $5,000.00
LYNN CANFIELD . . . . BERKELEY, CA 94

$100.00 WINNERS
1. Deborah A. Ahern . . . Atkinson, NH 03
2. Loma Andrus . . . . . .Huntsville, AR 72
3. Mrs. Charles Atkinson . . . .Warren, NJ
4.

2282 N. Beachwood
Los Angeles, California
90068 - ZIP CODE
January 2, 1978

President Richard M. Nixon
Casa Pacifica
San Clemente, California

Dear President Nixon,

Here's a picture I saw of
you in the National Inquir-
er. You're looking good!
Way better than the others!
I just thought perhaps you
would like to have it. It's
my pleasure - I just like to
do favors for people.

I was hoping to visit you
on the tour of your home
being sponsored by the San
Clemente Chamber of Commerce, but they sent the money
back and said they were all
filled up.
What I was wondering was if
maybe you could pull a few
strings and get me a couple
of tickets. I'm sure you
know people on the Chamber
of Commerce who you might be able to talk to.

I don't want you to think just because I sent
you the picture that you owe me anything, but
I'm sure someone like yourself knows how to
return a favor. One hand washes the other, am
I right? And I'm sure to you it's no trouble.

I am enclosing the money for the two tickets.
I don't want to make a big deal about it, but
if it's possible, could you try to get me two
tickets in the front of the bus. I like to
talk to the driver and learn as much as I can.

Many thanks. I know you're busy, but if it's
possible I hope we'll get a chance to meet.
Also I hope I get a chance to see your dogs!

Thanks a million!
I hope they have this tour <u>every</u> year!

Lazlo Toth
Lazlo Toth

HIGH PRIEST Om Prakash
Das has been standing day
and night for 15 years.

GURU Hari Das hasn't had
his hair cut for 50 years.

GOLFER: Richard Nixon
contemplates a putt at the
Shorecliffs Golf Club.

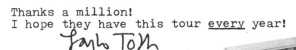

2282 N. Beachwood
Los Angeles, Calif.
90068 U.S.A.
January 3, 1978

Prime Minister Morarji Desai
Prime Minister's Home
New Delhi, India

Dear Prime Minister Desai,

Here's a picture I saw of you in
today's paper - I thought you might
enjoy showing it around New Delhi.

Please forgive this cold and very
blunt letter, but I am in a BIG
hurry. I am taking six puppies to
the Vet to get shots - but I know
you are busy, too, so I'll let you
go.

                Your friend,

                Lazlo Toth

                Lazlo Toth

POISED—Fly swatter about to strike.
AP Wirephoto

3 Swats and Out

NEW DELHI (UPI)—It was lunchtime. Indian Prime Minister Morarji Desai was President Carter's guest at the U.S. Embassy, but Carter was concerned about the man hovering behind him at the table.

The man was hard to ignore. He was swatting flies.

One lighted on the table.

The fly-swatter man's arm darted at his prey.

A miss.

Again.

Missed again.

Finally, success. The man reached over Carter's shoulder, collected the corpse, carried it off.

"That's the only thing they will show on the evening news," Carter cracked.

P.S. I read about a month ago in Time
magazine that you drink your own urine.
At first I thought to myself, "My God,
what will he think of next?" But then it explained how you
think it's good for you and that God said "Drink from your own
cistern", and it's free. The free part I understand, but when
God said that I thought he meant it spiritually, meaning we
should draw from our own inner strength. I think maybe the
Indian who translated it from the Hebrew must have mixed up
some words, just like when President Carter said he lusted after
the Polish people - it was just a bad translation! Anyway, I
must admit you look very good for your age. About how many
ounces do you think someone should try to begin with?

P.S.S. One more quick question: If urine is the water of life,
like you say, - what then is water?

Send me your picture!

DATE: January 3, 1978

TO: Foreign Affairs Advisor
ZABIGNEW ZABRINSKI
The White House
Washington, D.C.

FROM: Lazlo Toth
2282 N. Beachwood
Los Angeles, California
90068 - ZIPCODE

RE: President Carter's "sexual desire" for the Polish people.

A few years back, Ronald Ziegler, a former Presidential advisor, forgot to bring along the flag when President Nixon (Best!) went to Egypt - but this is worse! Much worse!
Don't get me wrong, I'm not saying that you are entirely to blame, but partly? No! More than partly? YES! I couldn't believe it when I heard on the news that you speak Polish! Why didn't you speak up and say something instead of letting the President of the United States make a fool of himself? Didn't you want to get involved? Don't you think something like this is like watching somebody get beat up in front of your house and not saying anything because you're too busy? The President of the United States got beat up (verbally) and you didn't raise a finger!

They call you the new Kissinger? Come on! Dr. Kissinger wouldn't have stood by and watched President Nixon's German translator make a fool out of him if it happened in Germany! He would have spoken up! In German and English! And then he would have made a nice joke out of it instead of making a joke out of the President! You just stood there looking like Dagwood Bumstead!
When the translator said the President had "sexual desires for the Polish people", and that he "abandoned the U.S.", didn't you think of speaking up? My God! Remember, the President of the U.S. represents all the American people, not just Democrats!

I didn't vote for President Carter, but I believe as President he deserves a competent staff at least. I'm glad President Carter let Bert Lance keep his diplomatic passport while he's working on selling his bank to the Arabs, so if he wants to fire any of you and hire him back he can get back here quick. At least Lance was a GENTLEMAN and was polite and took his medicine instead of zig-zagging around and putting the blame on others who don't even speak Polish!

Also, you might want to tell the President that I don't think it was very wise of him to make the crack about the fly swatter incident being the only thing covered in the press. I didn't hear him complaining when the press kept playing up President Ford's head bumping coverage! Or when they said President Nixon used to talk to paintings! He didn't go complaing then about Press coverage! I left the "n" out of complaining but I'm not even going back and correcting it - that's how I feel about it! You don't deserve it! When you see this letter you'll probably play dumb and say you don't read English! That's all! - for now,

Lazlo Toth

FRIENDLY REMINDER
PAYMENT IS
OVERDUE

2282 N. Beachwood
Los Angeles, California
90068 - ZIPCODE
July 16, 1978

President Richard M. Nixon
La Casa Pacifica
San Clemente, California

Dear Mr. President,

It was wonderful to see you on television when you went
down to Hyden, Kentucky, to get that sports complex named
after yourself. I think the speech you gave was one of
your all time greats! They just don't make Presidents like
they used to! (You can use that.)

I hate to loan people money because I hate to have to ask
for it back. So I hope you understand that this is a difficult
letter for me to write. (Five dollars may not seem much to
some people, but it can feed a dog for three weeks!)
I sent you $5 in January for two tickets to tour your home,
and I didn't get the tickets <u>or</u> the money back. I was really
looking forward to meeting you, but I understand,- you probably had other more important people you had to get tickets
for. And it was mostly my fault since I didn't even hear about
the tour until a few weeks after it was announced. Probably
if I told them I was a P.O.W. I could have gotten them. But
I didn't want to lie and that's why I sent the money to you
so you could make a few calls and get me the tickets. Anyway,
that's all over now, and if you would just return the money
everything will be fine. These things happen.

If I send you my copy of your book, would you sign it for me,
or do I have to get it from the publisher for $250? I will
pay postage both ways, this is my offer. I can't afford the
$250 deal - I'm not Rockefeller! (Do you get that one?) I
know you can take a joke because it says so in your book!

                    Nixon in '80!
                    America needs help!

                    Lazlo
                    Lazlo Toth

NO REPLY !

2282 N. Beachwood
Los Angeles, California
90068 - ZIPCODE
July 29, 1978

Hon. Edward R. Roybal
2404 Rayburn Office Building
Washington, D.C.   20515

Dear Congressman Roybal,

I was just going to write you again to see how the
new ethics code vote came out and then I read about
your being involved in Koreagate.
I personally don't see anything wrong with accepting
spending around money from Americans, but the fact
that it was from a foreign government kind of changes
things. The trouble is that someone may accuse you
of voting in favor of some bill that has to do with
Korea because Park gave you some money. That's the
problem.
I just wish that new ethics code was in effect a few
years ago, then none of this would have happened. Also
I bet it's mainly the anti-Korean congressmen who are
doing all the yelling. They're probably getting money
from Laos - you can never tell.

Anyway, I hope you got the raise and that you won't have
to take presents from other countries anymore. It's
expesive to live in Washington, and the people know it
because the paper regularily has a list of what different
foods cost in different cities and Washington is usually
higher than L.A. for just about everything except certain
vegtables - mainly because we grow them here and save
the shipping charges.

Here's a dollar for you to use however you want to. I
would say it was for your legal battle, but this way it
doesn't tie you down in any way.

                         Act confident!

                         Lazlo Toth
                         Lazlo Toth
                         25th District, California

     Encl: $1 American
            serial # L76796236G

EDWARD R. ROYBAL
25TH DISTRICT, CALIFORNIA

2404 RAYBURN OFFICE BUILDING
WASHINGTON, D.C. 20515
———
LOS ANGELES OFFICE:
ROOM 7106, NEW FEDERAL P.O. BLDG.
300 N. LOS ANGELES STREET
LOS ANGELES, CALIFORNIA 90012
PHONE: 688-4870

Congress of the United States
House of Representatives
Washington, D.C. 20515

August 11, 1978

COMMITTEE ON
APPROPRIATIONS

SUBCOMMITTEES:
LABOR-HEALTH EDUCATION AND
WELFARE
TREASURY-POSTAL SERVICE-GENERAL
GOVERNMENT
FOREIGN OPERATIONS

SELECT COMMITTEE ON AGING

CHAIRMAN-SUBCOMMITTEE ON
HOUSING AND CONSUMER INTERESTS

Mr. Lazlo Toth
2282 N. Beachwood
Los Angeles, California 90068

Dear Mr. Toth:

This will acknowledge and thank you for your recent
letter. Your dollar bill (serial # L76796236G) is
enclosed herewith.

Should you wish to correspond further on congressional
matters, your letters should be directed to Congressman
Henry Waxman. Congressman Waxman is the Member of
Congress who represents the district in which you reside.

It is, however, a pleasure to hear from you, as I am
aware of the great success you have achieved through your
correspondence with political figures.

Sincerely,

EDWARD R. ROYBAL
Member of Congress

ERR:as
Enclosure

2282 N. Beachwood
Los Angeles, California
90068 - ZIPCODE

August 8, 1978

Vice President in Charge of Radial Tires
Radial Tire Division
Firestone Rubber and Tire Company
Akron, Ohio

Dear Sir:

My Firestone Radial 500's have not blown up yet
and they will be <u>two</u> years old in November!

Just thought you'd like to hear from someone who
wasn't complaining.

                    Keep giving America a smooth ride!

                    Lazlo Toth

                    Lazlo Toth

PRESIDENT

August 24, 1978

Mr. Lazlo Toth
2282 N. Beachwood
Los Angeles, CA   90068

Dear Mr. Toth:

It was nice to read that your personal experience with our tires have given you good service and satisfaction. We know that a great many customers are getting good service from their Steel Belted Radial 500 tires -- over 660 billion miles of good service.

Too often today, people are quick to complain, and slow to compliment. Your kindness in writing about the good service that you received from your Firestone tires, is very much appreciated. Also, your loyalty to Firestone, is very much appreciated.

Sincerely,

M. DiFederico

MDiF/tmj

THE FIRESTONE TIRE & RUBBER COMPANY · 1200 FIRESTONE PARKWAY · AKRON, OHIO 44317

NO REPLY !

2282 N. Beachwood
Los Angeles, California
90068 - ZIP
U.S.A.
December 20, 1978

Deputy Prime Minister Teng Hsiao-ping
Deputy Prime Minister of China
c/o The Chinese Communist Party
Peking, China

Dear Deputy Prime Minister Teng,

On behalf of all the American people, I would like
to say that I hope we keep recognizing each other
for years to come!
You are a big country with almost a billion people
who need to buy everything, and we are a big country
who can sell it to you!

I would like to take this great moment and suggest
to you that in our hour of joy we not forget the one
man who made all this possible - President Richard
M. Nixon! He started the entire China-U.S. exchange,
and now you can repay him by suggesting to President
Carter that President Nixon be named Ambassador to
China! With China as his base, who knows what could
happen from there!

Also, I have read that the Coca-Cola Company is
planning on coming over to China. To this I say -
good! They are a fine company that have been around
for many years in this country and everybody seems to
like them.

I think you are one of the best leaders China ever
had!

America and China!
You need us, we need you!
Let's go!

Lazlo Toth

Lazlo Toth

LAZLO TOTH
2282 North Beachwood
Los Angeles, Calif. 90068

December 20, 1978

President J. Paul Austin
Chairman and Chief Executive Officer
Coca-Cola Company
Atlanta, Georgia

Dear Sir:

Welcome to China! Like all the newspapers say,
"it's a beginning of a new era for Coke!" There
are over 800,000,000 Chinese. If you could sell
just one Coke to each of them, you would sell
800,000,000 bottles of Coke. And that's if each
of them only bought one bottle each!

As an American, I am proud that the biggest and
best got in there instead of someone like RC or 7-Up.

Since you will be the biggest supplier of soft
drinks in that part of the world, President Carter
might be asking you for recommendations for
Ambassador to China, and a lot of Coca-Cola drinkers
are hoping you won't forget President Nixon.

I'll bet Mao is turning
over in his mausoleum!
(You can use that)

Lazlo Toth

Lazlo Toth

The Coca-Cola Company

ATLANTA, GEORGIA

J. PAUL AUSTIN
CHAIRMAN OF THE BOARD

ADDRESS REPLY TO
P. O. DRAWER 1734
ATLANTA, GA. 30301

404-897-2121

January 5, 1979

Mr. Lazlo Toth
2282 N. Beachwood
Los Angeles, California   90068

Dear Mr. Toth:

Thank you for your congratulations on
the China move. It was ten years in
the making, but I know it will be worth
it.

Kind regards.

Sincerely,

Paul Austin

JPA:lt

PAST DUE

2282 N. Beachwood
Los Angeles, California
90068 - ZIP CODE
December 21, 1978

President Richard M. Nixon (Roland)
La Casa Pacifica (The Pacific House)
San Clemente, California

Dear Mr. President,

Congradulations on the U.S. recognizing Red China.
It irks me to no end to see Carter standing there
taking all the credit and not even mentioning your
name - but I guess that's typical! In their hearts
the American people know who should get the credit,
and I'm sure the mail will be overwhelming asking
that you be named the new Ambassador to China. I'm
doing my share, that's for sure!

After the first of the year I plan on taking my
dogs and moving to New York for awhile. It's pretty
hard, with inflation the way it is, to keep a
possy of Dobbies like mine fed, and I've decided
that if I don't want to get rid of any of them I've
got to put them to work. I'll be going to Guard
Dog School with them, and when we come back I plan
to open my own business. The school in New York is
pretty expensive, so if you would send me the $5 I
sent you about a year ago I would appreciate it.
Every little bit helps! Also I'll be spending a
lot along the way because some motels make you pay
extra for each dog - this was just told to me recently.

I know that a new beginning for both of us is just
around the corner!

Onward to 1979!
The last year of the decade!
Let's go!

Laslo

Lazlo Toth

OFFICE OF RICHARD NIXON
LA CASA PACIFICA
SAN CLEMENTE, CALIFORNIA 92672

as requested

Interest

2282 N. Beachwood
Los Angeles, California
90068
January 20, 1981

President Ronald Reagan
President of the United States of America
The White House
Washington, D.C.

Dear President Reagan,

You can't imagine how long I've been waiting
to write those words! Finally that day has come!
The name "Reagan" right behind the name "President"!
Right where it belongs! I know that everything is
going to be fine again! Thank you!

This is your day!
This is your country!
This is my dream come true!

Lazlo Toth

Lazlo Toth

2282 N. Beachwood
Los Angeles, California
90068
January 25, 1981

Mrs. Nancy Davis Reagan
First Lady of The United States of America
The White House of the United States
Washington, D.C.

Dear Mrs. Reagan,

I always enjoyed looking at your picture in the paper
when you were just the first lady of California, but
now my wish has come true and you are First Lady of
all the land! You own some lovely gowns and the people
enjoy seeing them and hearing how much they cost -
thank you for bringing a little class and good grooming
back to America!

You and President Reagan are the best groomed and
classiest couple to live in the White House since
before the Fords, and I know you will help keep our
country number one again!

Welcome to the White House,
you deserve it!

Lazlo Toth

Lazlo Toth

February 23, 1981

Dear Mr. Toth:

I want you to know how much your thoughtful message meant to us. There is nothing that means more to my husband and me than knowing that we can count on the support and friendship of people like you.

With warmest regards,

Sincerely,

Nancy Reagan

NANCY REAGAN

We want you to know how much your message meant to us. There is much to do and we count on your support and friendship in our efforts to make that new beginning we all desire. With our heartfelt appreciation and best wishes,

Nancy and Ronald Reagan

The time
is now.
Reagan
Bush

2282 N. Beachwood
Los Angeles, California
90068
January 23, 1981

Vice President of the United States of America
George Herbert Walker Bush
c/o The White House
Washington, D.C.

Dear Vice President Bush,

First of all I want to say that I think you'll make
a good Vice-President even though you are somewhat
to the left of my personal preference. It's my wish
that some of President Reagan's sound thinking will
rub off on you and you'll see your way clear to veer
to the right a little if you're smart. As I understand it, President Reagan is thinking about not
running for re-election in '84, and if you play your
cards right, maybe Gov. Connally or General Haig or
whoever gets the presidential nomination, will choose
you for his running mate, too.

My main reason for this letter is to get history straight.
I have done some research in the field of Vice-President's
name lengths, and I've found that you have one of the
longest names of any V.P., although you also have one of
the shortest V.P. last names - tied with Burr and Ford.
Also, I found it interesting that President Reagan didn't
even use his middle name (Wilson) in his swearing in
ceremony, and you used <u>two</u> middle names! What gives?
I heard that President Reagan picked you because of
astrological reasons, and I figure that may be part of
your using all those names - am I right? I'll understand
if you don't want to answer such a personal question, but
I think you should since now all those names of yours are
part of the historical record, and you did want the job,
nobody talked you into it!

Keep up the good work! Keep up the good image of all of
us people with four letters in their last names!

                    Let's go America
                    Let's go Reagan and Bush!
                    Let's go!

                    Lazlo Toth

                    Lazlo Toth

OFFICE OF THE VICE PRESIDENT

WASHINGTON

1 March 1981

Mr. Lazlo Toth
2282 North Beachwood
Los Angeles, California 90068

Dear Mr. Toth:

Vice President Bush asked me to reply to your letter of 23 January.

This I do with considerable personal pleasure, for I am an avid fan of yours, having gone as far as to purchase a copy of your last book for use as a sort of counter-training manual in the Bush for President headquarters last year when I was in charge of answering the candidate's mail. Then there were many Lazlo Toth immitators; now that we are in the White House, we merit (and have received) the real thing.

If I may venture to correct something you said in your letter to Vice President Bush: There have been a total of four vice presidents with four-letter last names. In addition to Burr, Ford, and Bush there was William R. King, who was an aged senator from Alabama when Franklin Pierce selected him as his running mate in 1852. So sickly was King that Congress passed a special law permitting him to take the oath of office at the American consulate in Havana, where he had gone to recuperate from an illness. Duly sworn in, Vice President King returned to his home state to continue his recovery. But after only seven weeks in office, he died.

In his West Wing office, Mr. Bush has a portrait of President Pierce on the wall, a reminder of the dispensability of vice presidents.

Sincerely,

CHASE UNTERMEYER
Executive Assistant

2282 N. Beachwood
Los Angeles, California
February 25, 1981

Prince Charles Windsor
Prince of Whales
Buckingham Palace
London, England

Dear Prince Charles,

All I can say is, <u>It's About Time</u>! I can't tell you
how long all my friends and myself have been waiting
for you to get married.
I have this one friend especially who I meet everyday
at a coffee shop, and everyday I always ask him,
"Did you hear anything today?", and up till today he
always said, "no, not yet".
I feel terrible that I can't go down there today, but
I have to take my dogs to the vet.

Once I told my friend, "I know why he's waiting so
long to get married", and he said, "why?". I told
him, "He's waiting until he can collect social security!"
I know that since you're English you probably won't
get that, but what you have to know is that in order to
collect social security you have to be 65 years old!
I know it usually ruins a joke when you have to explain
it, but I figured if I didn't explain it you wouldn't
probably get it at all, and that would be worse. Plus
I know you probably have some American friends, and if
you tell them that joke I'll bet you'll find it works
pretty well.

I know that you and your Mom don't send out any pictures
of yourself, but since your future bride isn't royalty
yet, would it be possible to get a picture of her? Any
size will be fine.

                    Best regards to your entire
                    family from everyone in America,

                    Lazlo Toth
                    Lazlo Toth

BUCKINGHAM PALACE

10th April, 1981

Dear Laclo,

The Prince of Wales has asked me to write and thank you for your letter. His Royal Highness and the Lady Diana Spencer were delighted to receive your kind message of congratulations and have asked me to send you their very sincere thanks.

I am afraid however that it is not possible to send you a photograph. I am sure you will appreciate that it would not be possible to send photographs to the very many people who would like one. However, you could obtain such a photograph from: The Press Association Photos, 85 Fleet Street, London, E.C.4.

I am very sorry to have to send you this rather disappointing reply. Nevertheless His Royal Highness and the Lady Diana are most grateful for your thought in writing.

Yours sincerely,
Sonya Palmer.

Sonya Palmer

August 1, 1985
Post Office Box 245
Fairfax, Calif. 94930

Producers
60 Minutes
Sunday Night - 7 p.m.
CBS Television Network
New York, N.Y.

Dear Sirs,

If I may get right to the point -
Why do all the other people on your show get their
pictures on screen at the beginning and Andy Rooney
only gets his name mentioned but no picture of him
on the screen like the rest?

Even the newcomer, (Diane Sawyer) has her face on
screen and Rooney has been on for years. It's not fair
in my opinion and I would kindly request that you review
this situation in Mr. Rooney's favor.

Also, please repeat the show where Rooney talks about
how he likes to sneak into friends bathrooms and
surprize them by cleaning all their hair brushes and
combs. When they get home, all the brushes and combs
are clean and nobody knows who did it. It was one of
his all time bests, and I never saw it again.

        My best wishes to all the cast and crew,

                        Lazlo Toth

                        Lazlo Toth

P.S. What have you guys got against Rosano Brazzi?

CBS NEWS

A Division of CBS Inc.
524 West 57 Street
New York, New York 10019
(212) 975-4321

Memo to Letter Writers from Andy Rooney

There are good things and bad things about this recent well-knownness of mine. The money's good but there are problems. One of the problems is mail. I simply don't know what to do about it. I hate to think of all the people I've offended by not answering a letter they've sent me but I'm often getting as many as 100 letters a day. I hate answering letters anyway but even if I liked doing it, I couldn't answer 100 a day and do anything else.

This may be the most formless form letter you ever got but I'll tell you something I've thought about my mail for a couple of years now. We all make friends in different sections of our lives. We make them in grade school, high school and maybe college. We graduate, get married, take a job or move to another town and we make a whole new group of friends. We still like our old friends but our paths have diverged and we lose each other. We don't see our good old friends anymore. We make new friends and eventually part with them too. Our lives are compartmented and we have different friends in each compartment. No one can be friends all the time with all the friends he or she has made. Very often we lose track of them completely and can't even send them a Christmas card.

One of the best things about being in the public eye - and, believe me, there aren't many good things about it - is that my old friends can find me and write me. Them I write back. Everyone else who writes me a good letter makes me feel terrible because I have to send them this.

Forgive me,

[signature: Andy Rooney]

777 Center Blvd.
Fairfax, California
94930
Februry 5, 1987

Senator Lloyd Bentsen
c/o Senate Finance Committee
c/o U.S. Senate
Washington, D.C.

Dear Senator Bentsen,

I read in the newspaper yesterday about your
Breakfast Club and would be most interested
in being considered for membership.

As I understand it, you are asking $10,000
for the privilege of having breakfast with
you once a month for one year. That's twelve
breakfasts in all, or according to my arithmatic
about $835 per breakfast.

Now I would think for $835 you would be serving
eggs, a choice of ham, bacon or sausage, LARGE
juice, and an unlimited number of refills of
coffee.
I was wondering - IF I PROMISE TO ORDER ONLY
ONE PIECE OF TOAST AND ONE CUP OF COFFEE (no
refill), WHAT WILL IT COST ME? My friend told
me you'd probably still want $10,000, but I said
I'll bet you'd let me in the club for about
$5800, or about $480 per breakfast, a savings of
almost 50%. I am enclosing $1 American as a down
payment.

I'll bring my own jelly,

Lazlo Toth

Lazlo Toth

NO REPLY !

FIRST CLASS MAIL

General Delivery
Fairfax, California
USA   94930
June 10, 1987

Sultan of Brunei
Brunei - Northern Borneo

NO REPLY !

My Dear Sultan,

Forgive me if I have addressed you incorrectly,
but my dictionary does not provide information on how
to properly address a Sultan, so I had to take a stab
with "Dear" and hope it's not too personal.

I am writing to thank you for giving Lt. Col. Oliver
North, General Secord, Eliott Abrams and the rest the
ten million dollars for the Contras. And even though
they gave you the wrong Swiss bank account number and
you put the money in some stranger's account by mistake, it's the thought that counts and on behalf of
myself I would like to thank you anyway.

I don't know if you get CNN in Brunei, but that's
where I first heard about you. Then, the next week,
I read about you in PEOPLE magazine, congradulations!
Also congradulations on all those medals you were wearing in the picture. Lt. Col. Oliver North also has a
chest full of medals, but I would say you have more than
he does. I'm not sure, I haven't counted them, but my
impression is that you have more.

Sultan!, I must admit that I have another reason
for writing besides the Contra business. It's an in-
vestment proposition that I think may be right up your
alley. A 500 Hole Miniture Golf Course! It will be
the biggest minature golf course in the entire world!
I have had this idea for some time but have had a difficult time obtaining investors mainly because in the past
I have only tried to sell individual holes, you are the
first person I have approached with the proposition of
financing the entire project - all 500! As your 50-50
partner I would like to retain the rights to rent put-
ters and golf balls and in return all profits from coin
operated golf ball washers and cap rentals would be yours,
as well as a 50% interest in all the wind mill pumps and
other equipment we'll need to keep the place open 24 hours
a day, seven days a week, all year round.

It's just a little past midnight at my little oasis
here in California, my Sultan, but it's morning rise-and
shine time for you, so, GOODMORNING! How are you feeling
this morning, fine I hope!
I look forward to having you at my home someday for dinner.

All my best regards to everyone in Brunei,

Lazlo Toth

NO REPLY !

General Delivery
P.O. Box 245
Fairfax, California
94930 / USA
January 28, 1988

President Nicolae Ceausescu
President of Romania
ROMANIA

Dear Mr. President,

I knew your birthday was around now, but I wasn't
sure of the exact date, then I saw the enclosed
article in the newspaper and I knew I missed it
again. Sorry! But let me make up for it some by
saying those old standby words, BELATED HAPPY
BIRTHDAY! Stand up! You deserve it!

I guess in some circles it's a big deal to get a
birthday cards from the Queen of England, but I'm
surprized that someone with your world stature
could care less. Afterall, she didn't get <u>elected</u>
Queen. If her Father wasn't the King, she would
probably be working in some bakery somewhere, and
somebody would be telling her to please use a napkin
when she picks up the do-nuts to put them in the bag.

So, I hope in spite of this Queen business that you
had a nice Birthday,

Lazlo Toth

Lazlo Toth

February 5, 1988

Mrs. Raisa Gorbachev
c/o General Secretary Mikhail Gorbachev
The Kremlin
Moscow, Russia
USSR

Dear Mrs. Gorbachev,

First of all I'd like to apologize for taking so
long to write to thank you for visiting the USA last
December. I've been meaning to write for weeks,
but I've just been too busy, I'm sure you understand.
You don't celebrate Christmas over there, so you don't
have that excuse, but I had to put up the lights and
then take them down, which is two weeks right there,
plus a week to shop then a week to take back some gifts
I got that I didn't like, and then January is past
tense. Where does the time go? everybody says. I say,
where does the time come from, let me know that and
maybe we can figure out where it goes, do you get that
one?

Anyway, I hate to be the one to bring the enclosed
article to your attention, but it's better you hear it
from the common man instead of some insider in the
politbureau who would use it to try to unseat you husband
and put the hardliners back in power. I think the whole
thing has gone too far to send a thank-you at this late
date. My suggestion would be to call. I saw an add that
said if you call after 11 o'clock it's less than ten
dollars for three minutes, not that money is an object,
but just to point out nobody will be able to point at you
and call you some kind of soviet high roller, that's the
point I wanted to make by mentioning the price. Just
say I'm sorry I didn't write, I've been busy, that's it,
just get it over with and let's get on with the negotiations!

All my best regards to your husband,

Lazlo Toth

Lazlo Toth

NO REPLY !

P.O. Box 245
Fairfax, Calif. 94930
August 17, 1988

Senator Daniel Quale
Senator of the U.S. -State of Indiana
c/o U.S. Senate - U.S. Senate Building
Washington, D.C.

My Dear Quale,

Congrads are in order for your being chosen to be Bush's number two
man and none can be more joyous than yours truly.

You are a true conservative - one who puts what he says above what he
does, -and those who are throwing stones and hounding you just because
your Grandfather pulled a few strings to get you into law school because you
were such a terrible student will be eating crow when the Quale takes over
the new refurbished Vice President's office come January 1989.

In the past campaigns I have lent a hand to former Presidents Hoover,
Nixon, Ford, and Reagan, and I've decided, since I'm not too fond of the top
of our ticket - Bush is just too Texan for me, - to give a helping hand or two
to my new friend from the great heartland of our country - DANNY QUALE -
that's you! Stand up!

Now, Quale, I'm just starting out for you, and I hardly know you, nobody
does, so don't go looking for <u>perfection,</u> - but here are a couple IDEASTARTS,
as I call them, and I'll keep working on them until I get the go ahead or a
STOP from you or one of the top members of your staff.

Let's get to work! Here's a start of an idea for a stump speech:
Indiana is a nice place to go through if you have to drive from Washington to
Chicago, but I would want to drive there even if I wasn't going all the way to
Chicago - since I live there!. (Family angle)
I'll be expanding that idea plus this one:
Why do only kids have to say the Pledge of Allegiance in the morning?
Why don't you have Gumbold and Willard Scott say it on the TODAY SHOW,
so that everyone could start their day off right!

Let's have dinner together when you're in my district,

Lazlo Toth

Bush 88 Quayle

★ ★ ★ ★ ★ ★ ★ ★ ★ ★ ★ ★

October 5, 1988

Mr. Lazio Toth
P.O. Box 245
Fairfax, CA 94930

Dear Mr. Toth:

Thank you for taking the time to write. The letters of support Marilyn and I have received from across the country have been a great source of encouragement.

I agree with George Bush on the fundamental challenges facing this country, such as creating jobs, keeping taxes low, and increasing America's strength and security. Our priorities and values represent the mainstream of American life. Together we understand the importance not only of what has been accomplished, but what we <u>will</u> accomplish in the future.

Thank you again for the encouragement you have expressed for my family and me. I am pleased to know we can count on your support as we head toward November 8.

Sincerely,

Dan Quayle

733 15th Street, N.W. Suite 800 Washington, D.C. 20005 202/842-1988

Paid for by Bush–Quayle 88

L. TOTH
P. O. Box 245
Fairfax,
California
U. S. A. 94930

October 5, 1988

The Roman Curia
Sacred Department of Saints
The Roman Catholic Church
Vatican City, Vatican

Your Eminences:

I would like to report a miracle to Fr. Junipero Serra.

Do I have to fill out some kind of form now or what?

Best regards to His Holiness and his staff.

Lazlo Toth

Lazlo Toth

CONGREGAZIONE
PER LE CAUSE DEI SANTI

Rome, October 25, 1988

Dear Mr. Toth,

Your letter of October 5th has arrived at this Congregation for the Causes of the Saints in which you speak of a "miracle" granted through the intercession of Blessed **JUNIPER SERRA.**

As only one canonically approved miracle is required for his canonization, this "miracle" of which you speak must have occurred on or after the date of beatification, that is, September 25, 1988. If this be the case, I would advise you to send a report of the "event" to the Bishop of the diocese where it took place so that he may consider initiating a canonical investigation or not.

With every best wish, I am

Sincerely in Christ,

+ Traian Crisan

Archbishop Traian Crisan
S e c r e t a r y

Post Office Box 245
Fairfax, California 94930
October 11, 1988

Sen. Lloyd Bentsen
c/o U.S. Senate
Washington, D.C.

Dear Senator,

Here's a dollar, please send me a button, Dukakis
and Bentsen for President, I collect them.

You did a fine job in the debate, but you shouldn't
have said that about Senator Quale not being another
President Kennedy, that was uncalled for.

How tall are you?

If you and Dukakis get elected do you think they'll
be a place for Maureen Reagan in the administration?
I know she's a Republican, but think of her experience.

November 8, election day, is only three weeks ahead of
us but it feels like it's sneaking up from behind!

Lazlo Toth

Lazlo Toth

Dukakis/Bentsen

499 South Capitol St., S.W., Washington, DC 20003
(202) 863-1445   FAX (202) 488-4826

October 18, 1988

Mr. Lazlo Toth
Box 245
Fairfax, CA 94930

Dear Mr. Toth:

Thank you for your support and good wishes.

I am very pleased and honored to be on the ticket
with Governor Dukakis and I sense a renewed unity
in the Democratic Party.

This is a crucial election for our country. The
support and advice of friends like you is
encouraging and valuable.

Thanks again.

Sincerely,

Lloyd Bentsen

NO REPLY !

Box 245 / Fairfax, California / 94930
October 10, 1988

Senator Daniel J. Quayle
733 15th Street, N.W. Suite 800
Washington, D.C. 20005

My Dear Quayle,

First of all I want to say I'm sorry I misspelled your name, and second of all I'd like to point out that you did the same with mine. I guess neither of us is Daniel Webster! Do you get that one?

Well! You sure came though with flying colors in the debate with Benson! You made him look like mince meat! After he said to you, "Senator, you're no John Kennedy", you gave him that stare of yours and coupled it with that great remark, "Senator, that was uncalled for".   You blasted him out of the water with that one! The Benson ship goes down!
And how about how you kept putting down the liberal Dukakis! My friends and I were sure impressed. The only mistake I made was I forgot to tape it! Do you think Marilyn could run me off a few VCR copies? I'll be needing the video tape to show it to people who missed the debate when it was on the tube. I plan to start campaigning , door to door, on your behalf, in about a week . I'm almost done painting the porch and then as soon as I get done painting the garage , I'll get out there.

Frankly, I ran into some concept problems on the FAMILY ANGLE SPEECH, but I've been spending a lot of my time on the Pledge thing and I hope you're sitting down because here comes an idea of a lifetime!
Every morning, seven A.M. sharp, I always say the Pledge of Allegience on the phone, with my friend, George Tuttle. That's how I got the idea:
<u>How about RECORDING the Pledge of Allegience and putting it on a 900 telephone line and have people pay two dollars to say the Pledge along with you and George Bush!</u> It's a great way to pay off some of the campaign expenses, plus it will stop all the rumors that George Bush doesn't want to be seen with you, - he'll have to get together with you at the recording session! Naturally, I'd like to be in on this, do you think you and George could fit it into your schedules to record the Pledge in my area? or I could meet you guys in New Orleans or someplace that's convenient to all of us.
I'm sending a dollar for a button so I'll have something official to wear when I'm canvassing my area.

I love you,

Lazlo Toth

POBox 245, Fairfax, California, 94930
November 9, 1988

President- Elect
George Herbert Walker Bush III Jr.
c/o The White House
Washington, D.C.

Dear President-elect Bush,

    Congradulations are in order - you won! Soon it will be President Bush!
The first President with four letters in his last name since President Ford!
Some may say your election wasn't a mandate, but I say, "No, it was a
mandate!" If you say it was a mandate, it's a mandate! You're the President,
you can call it whatever you want! Personally, I think it was a kinder,
gentler mandate than the usual mandate, but just the same, it was a
mandate. And that was even with Dansworth J. Quale on the ticket! Without
Quale, it would have been a real mandate, everybody knows that.

    To make a long story short, I never got the button <u>or</u> the balloon! To tell
you the truth, I didn't have much hope of ever receiving the button after
Marilyn Quale failed to send me the video tape like she was suppose to, so
that was a sign to me that I shouldn't count on receiving a button, but I
really thought I'd get the balloon since it was coming directly from your
headquarters. I guess you were too busy in those closing days of the
campaign with the zip code problem. Anyway, why I'm writing is to say I
hope your people don't feel that they have to still send the balloon now, it
would just be a waste of postage, what good is it going to do me now? It's
too late now!
    I guess I could keep it for '92, but what if Quale's name is on the balloon,
too? You probably won't be running with him next time, considering he
almost made you lose. I heard somebody say that he's giving C students a
bad name. Why don't they ever mention that he's a very good A plus golfer!
Why do they always just mention the negative?

    I hear that you're going to go to Florida to fish. That's good, you need all
the rest you can get now, pretty soon you're going to have to start dealing
with the <u>E</u> word - the <u>E</u>conomy! Do you get that one?
    I hope you won't forget President Nixon when it comes time for you to
name your new Ambassador to China.

    Let me know if I can be of any help during the transition,

Lazlo Toth

Lazlo Toth

Gy Bush   Barbara Bush

Jack MacDonough

BUY AMERICAN

P.O. Box 245
Fairfax, California 94930
November 15, 1988

President
Anheiser - Bush Company
St. Louis, Missouri

Dear Mr. President,

I used to occasionally drink your BUDWEISER Brand, that's how I know the name of your company, and all the fine products you make, light as well as Dark.

I have a marketing idea that goes with your name since you have the same name as our new President, George Bush.

Since he wants a "kinder, gentler nation", I thought up the idea for you to sell a new beer,- BUSH BEER - A KINDER, GENTLER BEER .

Maybe it should be BUSH LIGHT, I'll leave that up to you, you're the beer experts, I just come up with the ideas.

I'll settle for half a cent a bottle or can - or 2 1/2 cents for a six pack (a half cent discount on my side) and I'll donate half of what I make to President Bush to help pay off the deficit. I think it's a great marketing gimmick to let people know that everytime they're drinking a BUSH BEER they're helping to pay off the nation's deficit.

And here's another line I just came up with to show you I have more than one:

Don't drink and drive -
Drink and pay off the deficit!
DRINK BUSH BEER!
A kinder, gentler beer!
And take a cab.

I know it's not much time, but it sure would be nice to have this stuff on the shelves by Inauguration Day, Jan. 20, 1989. Don't give me the "we can't do it that fast" excuse, -we've got more than two months, plenty of time! Don't forget, the advertising line is already done, we've just got to get the lawyers going with the contracts on your end. Should I fly there to sign the papers or do you just want to mail them to me?

My social security number is available upon request,
but I hope I'm not going to have to pay taxes on this,

Lazlo Toth

Lazlo Toth

RECEIVED

NOV 2 1 1988

OFFICE OF
AUGUST A. BUSCH III

65

Anheuser-Busch, Inc.
ONE OF THE ANHEUSER-BUSCH COMPANIES

December 9, 1988

Mr. Lazlo Toth
P.O. Box 245
Fairfax, CA   94930

Dear Mr. Toth:

Thank you for contacting us regarding your idea.

As you are probably aware, Anheuser-Busch retains the services
of many creative sources. These sources provide us with many
ideas and concepts. Some are used; some put on the shelf for
future consideration; and there are many that are never used at
all. In addition to these agency sources, Anheuser-Busch
receives thousands of ideas from people like yourself each
year. As I'm sure you can appreciate, the likelihood is very
small that such an unsolicited idea would be accepted.

In keeping with company policy, we cannot accept unsolicited
ideas on a confidential basis. Before considering an idea
submitted by an individual outside the company, we ask that
person to sign one copy of the enclosed agreement, keep one for
his or her records, and return a copy to the undersigned, along
with a description of the concept/idea. Once this is done, the
appropriate department will evaluate the proposal and determine
our interest in it.

Because each of the ideas we receive is given individual
consideration, we anticipate that it will be approximately four
to five weeks from the date we receive your release before we
are able to reply to your proposal. Accordingly, we ask that
you be patient during this period.

Sincerely,

Jack MacDonough

Jack MacDonough
Vice President - Brand Management

Enclosures

Anheuser-Busch, Inc.
One Busch Place
St. Louis, MO U.S.A. 63118-1852
Telex 447 117 ANBUSCH STL

P O Box 245
Fairfax, California
U S A 94930
November 17, 1988

Prime Minister Margaret Thratcher
10 Downing Street - Buckingham Palace
London, England - Great! Britain

My Dear Prime Minister,

It was wonderful to see you at the State Dinner at the White House.
I know you and the President had lots to reminisce about.   Such evenings
always seem to be over too quick, and all too soon you'll have nobody to
chew the fat with except Bush and Quale. They're not bad company, I'm told,
but they're no Gipper, we know that!

You looked lovely in that dress with the big shoulders and the pleats.
I saw Oprah Winfry wearing a dress that looked like that on T.V. awhile
back, but she could never wear it now!   She says she lost 80 pounds by
going on some total liquid (no chew) diet, but I saw a magazine in the
grocery store that said what she really did to lose all that weight was to have
her head transplanted on some other woman's body . It said she got it done
in Mexico and that it cost $300,000, not including transportation from
Chicago, that was extra!

Madame Prime Minister, I am putting together a book to give to the
President when he leaves office come January 20th.   I'm asking friends of
his to send a picture of themselves holding a hat in their laps. The name of
the book is HATS OFF TO YOU, MR. PRESIDENT, or Mr. PRESIDENT, HATS OFF
TO YOU, I'm not sure , yet.
Please send the picture as soon as possible. I know the President will be
especially happy when he seees you in there! Everyone knows he likes you
even more than the Queen. So, hat's off to you, too! And here's hoping we
can keep the great alliance betwwen our two nations intact under the Bush-
Quale administration!

Somebody told me once we're probably distant cousins,

Lazlo Toth

Lazlo Toth

1O DOWNING STREET
LONDON SW1A 2AA

From the Private Secretary   5 December 1988

Dear Mr. Toth,

    I am writing on behalf of the Prime
Minister to thank you for your letter
of 17 November concerning your proposed
book to present to President Reagan.

    I very much regret it will not be
possible for Mrs. Thatcher to help in
the way you suggest since we only have
the official photograph of her.

    I am sorry to send you this disappointing
reply, but do hope you will understand.

Yours Sincerely,

Tessa Gaisman

MRS. TESSA GAISMAN

Mr. Lazio Toth

NO REPLY !

P.O. Box 245 / Fairfax, California
94930 USA
1 December 1988

General Augusto Pinochet
Headquarters of the Chief/General/CEO
Santiago, CHILI

My dear General Pinochet,

Ola! Amigo! Bravo!

As I'm sure you're aware, President Reagan, like yourself, will be leaving office soon. In no time at all he'll be sitting in front of his fireplace in Beverly Hills, looking though the book I'm preparing right now.

My Dear General, you have been selected by yours truly, along with the Knights of Malta, among others, to participate to the fullest extent!

My General, My Pinochet, the name of the book is:
<u>HATS OFF TO YOU, MR. PRESIDENT</u>, or, <u>MR. PRESIDENT, HATS OFF TO YOU,</u>
I'm not sure yet.

My request, - Please send a photograph of yourself with your hat in your hand - or your lap if you prefer.

Muchas gracias,
I eat your peppers!

Lazlo Toth

Lazlo Toth

Box 245 / Fairfax, California / 94930
December 10, 1988

Secretary of Energy John S. Herrington
Department of Energy
Washington, D.C.

Dear Secretary of Energy Herrington,

I see in this morning's paper that you awarded the Bechtel Group of San Francisco a one billion dollar contract to develop a system to transport and store radioactive wastes. The article says Bechtel's responsibilities include developing an environmentally safe method for collecting waste at nuke plants, transporting it to a geologically stable area and storing it under the ground for long enough to render it harmless - a period of "about" 10,000 years.

Since Bechtel is responsible for storing the waste for about 10,000 years, it just doesn't seem right to me to pay them the whole amount until the job is completed! What if about 5,000 years from now some of that stuff starts leaking out? It will be almost impossible to collect for damages after that amount of time! They'll say they "Don't recall"! And who knows if Bechtel will still even be in business! They'll have probably been taken over by Philip Morris or Proctor and Gamble, or somebody like that by then!

My suggestion:
Why don't we pay a fair fee now up front, say half a billion dollars, but then let's spread the other half a billion out over the duration of the project - about 10,000 years.

Probably as Secretary of Energy you'll be able to handle this yourself, but maybe this is something Vice President Quale can get involved with. President -Elect Bush is looking for something for Quale to do since they won't let him be the Drug Czar and if he could be involved with saving the American people half a billion dollars, it would be good for his image. And if you could help him figure out why it is that Man's body decomposes in a matter of months, but the waste that he makes lasts 10,000 years, and turn the situation around, you would be a real hero to a lot of people for years to come.

It may just be ten thousand years for us,
but for a dog it's seventy thousand years!

Lazlo Toth

Department of Energy
Washington, DC 20585

JAN 2 3 1989

Mr. Lazlo Toth
P.O. Box 245
Fairfax, California 94930

Dear Mr. Toth:

Thank you for your letter of December 10, 1988, to
Secretary Herrington concerning the Department of Energy's (DOE)
selection of Bechtel Systems Management, Inc., for the overall
management of DOE's program for the safe disposal of radioactive
waste.

I have enclosed a copy of DOE's press release which describes the
selection of Bechtel for contract negotiation and clarifies
Bechtel's role in the high-level nuclear waste disposal program.
DOE will conduct its program activities related to waste disposal
in full compliance with the Nuclear Regulatory Commission and
Environmental Protection Agency regulatory and environmental
requirements. DOE will reimburse Bechtel for costs incurred in
managing the program for the 10-year contract period, plus DOE
will award a fee to Bechtel based strictly on their performance.
This contract arrangement assures DOE of a cost-effective approach
to management of the nuclear waste disposal program.

Thank you for your interest in the high-level nuclear waste
disposal program.

Sincerely,

Stephen H. Kale
Associate Director for
   Facilities Siting and Development
Office of Civilian Radioactive
   Waste Management

Enclosure

TO: Mr. Jack MacDonough
Vice President
Anheuser-Bush, Inc.
St. Louis, MO.

December 14, 1988

Re: President Bush Beer
A kinder, gentler beer.

I, _____LAZLO HOOVER TOTH_____, have
read the following conditions, and I indicate my acceptance of
said conditions and request that Anheuser-Busch Companies, Inc.,
its subsidiaries and affiliates, hereinafter referred to as
Anheuser-Busch, consider my above-referred-to idea in view of my
acceptance of said conditions.

1. The submission of my suggestions or ideas (as well as any
additional ones which I may hereafter submit as incidental to the
material originally submitted) shall not be in confidence or
establish a confidential relation between me and Anheuser-Busch.

2. Anheuser-Busch makes no commitment that the ideas or
materials submitted shall be kept secret.

3. Any consideration which Anheuser-Busch gives my ideas or
materials shall be without obligation of any kind assumed by or
implied against Anheuser-Busch, unless and until such obligation
is expressed in a formal written contract executed by a duly
authorized officer of Anheuser-Busch under its corporate seal.

4. I do not grant to Anheuser-Busch any rights under any patent
or trademark or copyright registration which I now have or may
later obtain covering the subjects which I submit; but, in
consideration of examination by Anheuser-Busch of my suggestions
or ideas, I release Anheuser-Busch from any and all liability
because of its use of all or any portion thereof, except such
liability as may arise by reason of valid patents now or
hereafter issued or valid trademark or copyright registrations
which I now or hereafter may own.

5. I get 2 1/2 ¢ per six pack .

Signature Line _____Lazlo Toth_____

Printed Name _____TOTH LAZLO_____

Address _____PO BOX 245 FAIRFAX_____
_____CALIFORNIA, 94930_____

Date _____DECEMBER 14, 1988_____

2220S

ANHEUSER-BUSCH COMPANIES   Legal Department

January 26, 1989

Mr. Lazlo Hoover Toth
P.O. Box 245
Fairfax, CA 94930

Dear Mr. Toth:

Jack MacDonough has referred your advertising idea and release form, dated December 14, 1988, to me.

You have amended our standard agreement. Since we do not accept unsolicited ideas unless our agreement is signed as is, and not with any amendments or revisions, I am returning your idea and release.

It is unfortunate that you feel that our standard agreement is not in your best interest. I can assure you that we deal with all proposals in a fair manner. To do otherwise would be extremely shortsighted on our part.

If you wish to resubmit your idea, please sign one copy of the enclosed agreement, and return it to me along with the description of your idea. The additional copy is for your records.

Because each of the ideas we receive is given individual consideration, we anticipate that it will be approximately four to five weeks from the date we receive your release before we are able to reply to your proposal. Accordingly, we ask that you be patient during this period.

Thank you for contacting Anheuser-Busch. We appreciate your interest in our company.

Sincerely yours,

Kathy Toczylowski

Kathleen R. Toczylowski
Legal Assistant

enclosures

3453S

Anheuser-Busch Companies, Inc.
Executive Offices
One Busch Place
St. Louis, MO U.S.A. 63118-1852
Telecopier (314) 577-3835

245 Post Office Box
Fairfax, California USA 94930
27 December 1988

Prime Minister Margaret Thratcher
Buckingham Palace
10 Downing Street
London SW1A 2AA England

My Dear Prime Minister,

I received a letter from your private secretary, Mrs. Tessa Gaisman, who said the only photograph you can send is your "official" one.

I guess you're too busy what with the Holidays and all to take one special for President Reagan at this time.
It would only take a few minutes, but that's your decision.
You know more than anyone all that he's done for you, so you must be especially busy not to be willing to take the few minutes it would take to have the picture taken.

I know how disappointed he's going to be when he realizes you're not in there with Prime Minister Mulrooney, Kurt Waldheim, Jane Wyman , and the rest. So I've been thinking this over and I've decided that since the name of the book is: <u>Hats off to you, Mr. President,</u> or, <u>Mr. President , Hats off to you,</u> your official photograph should work just fine, just as long as you're not wearing a hat in it.   But , if you're wearing a hat in the official photograph, I'm afraid I'm going to have to pass.

In just a matter of days it will be a New Year! 1989 they will call it! And only 20 days later our Gipper will leave office, - and I want the book in his <u>hands</u> by then, not in the <u>mail,</u> so - Let's go!
Don't let the English people down!

Your toffee still sells well here at Christmas time,

Lazlo Toth

Lazlo Toth

1O DOWNING STREET

LONDON SW1A 2AA

From the Private Secretary   10 January 1989

Dear Mr. Toth,

    The Prime Minister has asked me to
thank you for your further letter of 27 December.
I am afraid that, as you will understand,
the demands on the Prime Minister's time
are really very onerous and it will not
be possible for her to pose for a special
photograph. We have had to turn down
so many similar requests but I am sorry
to bring a disappointing reply.

Yours sincerely,

Tessa Gaisman

<u>Mrs T Gaisman</u>

Mr. Lazlo Toth

P.O. Box 245
Fairfax, California
9 4 9 3 0
April 2, 1989

President
Pepsi Cola Company
Pepsico, Inc.
Purchase, NY

Dear President of Pepsi,

My church group tells me that if enough people such as myself write to you and complain about your commercial with MADONNA, you will cave in and take the commercial off the air.

I haven't seen the commercial myself yet, but I understand it's pretty disgusting! They say she's wearing just a slip!

So, please, take the Madonna commercial off the air! If you don't, everyone I know will stop buying Pepsi Cola and switch to R.C. Cola or Dr. Pepper or maybe even Coca-Cola!

I understand you people also own Fritos. That's a fine snack and I sure wouldn't want to see it dragged into this Madonna business, but if something doesn't happen quick, this boycott could spread.

Have you folks ever thought about marketing a totally flat Pepsi for those of us who don't think it's morally right to consume a fully carbonated refreshment? Now we have to shake the bubbles out ourselves, and it can be quite embarrassing at social occasions. If you were to come out with a totally non carbonated Cola, you could sew up the whole market! Think it over.

I'll be drinking V-8 juice until my prayers are answered,

Lazlo Toth

Lazlo Toth

PEPSI-COLA COMPANY **PEPSI** SOMERS, NEW YORK 10589

April 25, 1989

Mr. Lazlo Toth
P.O. Box 245
Fairfax, CA94930

Dear Mr. Toth:

Thank you for taking the time to share your concerns with us regarding
Pepsi's use of Madonna in one of our commercials. Your letter was
referred to me, since my office serves as a liaison for communicating to
management the very important public opinion expressed in letters such as
yours.

As you may already be aware, we have decided against featuring Madonna in
any further advertising. That decision was made in response to concerns
expressed by you and other consumers, in light of the confusion
surrounding the commercial.

Pepsi-Cola has a history of promoting its products with highly creative
and entertaining advertising, featuring some of the most popular
performers of the day. That was our intent when we signed Madonna to
appear in a commercial which would also premiere her new song, "Like A
Prayer".

However, the day after our new commercial debuted, Madonna released a
separate music video for the same song. The video, which we wish to
stress is totally unrelated to our commercial, has generated a great deal
of speculation and controversy, and has frequently been confused with our
ad.

We deeply regret that this situation occurred, but we sincerely appreciate
the fact that so many people have chosen to communicate their opinions to
us. It is extremely important to Pepsi that the celebrities who sometimes
represent our products serve to enhance the positive image that has helped
make Pepsi one of the world's most popular consumer products. Please be
assured that we will do everything in our power to continue that tradition.

I hope that you'll agree that the actions we've taken have been the
appropriate ones, and also that I may have helped to clarify the situation
to some degree. In either event, thank you for writing to us; we regret
that events caused you concern and we hope the enclosed coupon for our
products will begin to restore your confidence in us. We value your
opinion highly.

Sincerely,

Christine Jones
Consumer Affairs

P. O. Box 245
Fairfax, California 94930
USA
April 6, 1989

Prime Minister Margaret Thratcher
Buckingham Palace
10 Downing Street
London SW1A 2AA England

Dear Prime Minister,

Good news! I've decided to change the name of the book! I'm going to call it: <u>We salute you, Mr. President!</u>, or, <u>Mr. President, a salute from us!</u> I'm still not sure which title I'll use, but at the moment I'm leaning towards the second one, it seems warmer.

So , as you can see, it really doesn't matter anymore if you're wearing a hat or not in the photograph! Even if you have a hat on in your official photo - it doesn't matter, don't worry about it, it will do just fine!
If, just by luck, you may happen to have a photo of yourself in which you are saluting, that would be perfect, but the official one will be fine, too.

Everything is going quite smoothly on this end. I think the name change was a good idea, even though it may seem strange because most of the people will be holding their hats in their hands in the photos. But, if that's the way it has to be, that's the way it has to be, I'm willing to do it for you, you're worth it.

I know I'm getting the book to our President a little late, but I'm waiting for a few other last minute stranglers to come in besides yourself. It's understandable why I haven't heard from General Pinochet, what with the cyanide grape boycott problem and all, but I don't know what excuse the Pope has got. Maybe he's been traveling again.

My time is onerous, too!
The English language- Best!

Lazlo Toth

Lazlo Toth

Sorry it's taken me so long to write.

L. Toth
P. O. Box 245
Fairfax,
    California
U. S. A. 94930

October 24, 1990

Archbishop Traian Crisan
Secretary
Congregation for the Causes of the Saints
Vatican City
The Vatican

Your Eminence,

I'm sorry it's taken me so long to get back to you regarding the Father **Junipero Serra** miracle that happened on **Route 280** when I was on my way to Gilroy on September 24, 1988, but I am in somewhat of a dilemma, and before pursuing this cause further I was wondering how locked in you are to the September 25th date or if there might be some kind of a waiver in a case like this, what with only a twenty four hour time difference.

Also, do you have some kind of a Report of Miracle form, or some kind of instructions to follow? I don't know how detailed you want me to get at this time.

I look forward to working closely with the canonical investigation team and am willing to meet them at the airport if desired.

Regards and best wishes to everyone you know ,

Lazlo Toth

Lazlo Toth

TO: The President
      McDonald's Hamburgers Company
      World Headquarters
      Oak Brook, Illinois 60521

FROM: Lazlo Toth
      P. O. Box 245
      Fairfax-94930-Calif.
      <u>November 6, 1990</u>

<u>Yesterday</u> I ordered a Filet-O-Fish sandwich and small French Fries at your restaurant on the Miracle Mile near San Rafael and paid $2.49 at the drive-up window. I have no idea why they call it the Miracle Mile, but that's what they call it.

At the window (#2), your employee handed me a bag that said, "McRib Pack" on it. I said I didn't order "McRib's" but she said that was just "writing on the bag", and that even though the bag said "McRib Pack"on it , no McRibs were involved - just a Fish Sandwich and French Fries. I figured you must have been out of Filet-O-Fish bags. But when I got home and opened the bag, all that was inside was four paper napkins and one Filet-O-Fish sandwich! No french fries! The French Fries were missing! I paid for them, but they were not there!

Either they fell out of the bag or I was cheated, and I don't see how they could fall out of the bag! It was in my car the whole time! I'm sure they didn't cheat me on purpose, but I was cheated out the French Fries just the same - I don't have them! You do! And I paid for them! Cash! It doesn't cost $2.49 just for a Filet-O-Fish! Come on!

I tried to telephone them to report it and they're NOT LISTED! Other McDonald's restaruant were listed, but not THEM! Why aren't they listed? What are they afraid of? I had to call Kinney Shoes next door and have them send someone over to McDonald's to tell them about what happened. Then I got cut off, and when I tried to call back, it was always busy.

Please send my French Fries to the above address and I suggest you tell your employees to cut down on the napkins! They act like everybody orders the McRibs! Maybe if they weren't so busy giving away free napkins and the wrong bags they would have remembered the french fries!

Lazlo Toth

P.S. A friend of mine used to work at McDonald's and then he switched to Jack-in-the-Box and now a lot of people say he's much happier. How much this is due to his job change and how much is due to other factors in his life, -this I do not know. All I know is everybody say's he happier.

McDonald's Corporation
2480 North First Street
Suite 220
San Jose, California 95131-1002
408/922-0990

November 19, 1990

Mr. Lazlo Toth
P. O. Box 245
Fairfax, CA   94930

Dear Mr. Toth:

Thank you for taking the time to write to McDonald's. Please accept our
sincere apology for any inconvenience you may have experienced.

McDonald's does its best to maintain high standards of quality, service,
cleanliness, value and courteous service to insure that each visit you make to
one of our restaurants is a pleasant one. Customer satisfaction is one of our
top priorities, and we are concerned and interested whenever a customer is
dissatisfied for whatever reason.

I have brought this situation to the attention of the franchisee who owns that
particular McDonald's, and feel confident that the matter will be corrected.
Please accept the enclosed Be Our Guest cards for your use on future visits to
any McDonald's restaurant.

Again, thank you for sharing your thoughts with us. Through your comments we
learn how to serve you better.

Very truly yours,
McDONALD'S CORPORATION

Joan Qui Henry
Public Relations Coordinator

/sjb

FILET-O-FISH®

Present this card at McDonald's®. It entitles you to one of our
tender Filet-O-Fish sandwiches, served with cheese and tartar
sauce all on a steamed bun.
Limit One Coupon Redeemable Per Customer Per Visit. Not Good in Conjunction
with Any Other Offer. Cash Value 1/20 of 1¢. Void Where Prohibited.
REDEEMABLE ONLY AT McDONALD'S   +

Any Participating McDonald's

EXPIRES† 2-1-91   BY†

Operator for reimbursement send to: McDonald's Corporation,
2480 N. First St., Suite 220, San Jose, CA 95131-1002
†Void if blank. Present card before ordering. ©1990 McDonald's Corp. 35 475.2

MEDIUM ORDER OF FRENCH FRIES

Present this card at McDonald's®. It entitles you to a medium
order of crisp, golden-brown French Fries. This is our way of
acquainting you with McDonald's great taste and quick
service.
Limit One Coupon Redeemable Per Customer Per Visit. Not Good in Conjunction
with Any Other Offer. Cash Value 1/20 of 1¢. Void Where Prohibited.
REDEEMABLE ONLY AT McDONALD'S   +

Any Participating McDonald's

EXPIRES† 2-1-91

Operator for reimbursement send to: McDonald's Corporation,
2480 N. First St., Suite 220, San Jose, CA 95131-1002
†Void if blank. Present card before ordering. ©1990 McDonald's Corp. 35 475.6

BE OUR GUEST

President George Bush
The White House
Washington, D.C. USA (Best!)

December 17, 1990

My President!

You have given Sandman Insane (that's what I call him) until January 15, to get out of Kuwait, and, my President, I can't wait!

We've got him up against the sand bags now, because I know you won't back down. No way! And I loved it when you said, "If we start a war, it won't be another Viet Nam!". Does this mean it will be another Hiroshima? Are we going to bomb them to oblivion and wipe them off the map of the planet Earth? That's what it sounds like you're saying to me, and I'm one American who say's, - Mister President, Go! Go! Go!, what's the holdup?, bombs away! Let's show them who runs the world! America!, that's who! Like the cheer says, "Everywhere we go, people want to know, who we are, so we tell them! "America!, number one! We don't give everybody money for nothing! If other countries don't like it, they could pay up or shut up, nuts to them!

We could have blockaded Japan too, but it would have taken MONTHS!, maybe even a YEAR! to accomplish what two little bombs did in MINUTES! BOOM! = SURRENDER! You know that! GO! Go! Go! Bombs away!

BUT, my President, here is an alternative plan if the peace niks and chicken draftable college students and their mothers start "protesting" and cause the press to start saying that you can't be reelected in '92 if you drop a few big ones and kill and maim a lot of "innocent" people (arab shields).

Why not propose to Saddam that, as a solution to the problem, Kuwait be turned into a homeland for the Palestinians? It would really call Saddam's bluff! He wants to link Kuwait with the Middle East problem, - here's his chance to prove it! World opinion, and the other Arabs! would force him to go for the idea, and it would solve the middle east problem once and for all!

Think it over. Dream on it. Talk it over with Sunnunu and James Baker and the folks at Exxon. That's my request.

Merry Christmas!
Peace on Earth -until Jan. 15th!

Lazlo Toth

Lazlo Toth

The President and Mrs. Bush
extend their warmest wishes
for a merry Christmas
and a new year that will bring
harmony to our world
and happiness to you
and those you love.

1990

P.O. Box 245
Fairfax, California
94930 USA!

February 28, 1991

J. Paul Austin
Chairman of the Board
The Coca-Cola Company
P. O. Drawer 1734
Atlanta, GA. 30301

Dear Paul,

   I just heard on CNN that some of our Marines were just dropped by
helicopter into our embassy in Kuwait, and, fortunately, they reported back
that the building wasn't damaged too badly. But!, they said there was
evidence that the enemy was in there because, "the Coca-Cola machine was
all busted up".

   Why don't we get a new one over there right away.

                    All the best,

                    Lazlo

                    Lazlo Toth

THOMAS E. GRAY
DIRECTOR, EXTERNAL AFFAIRS
NORTHEAST EUROPE/AFRICA GROUP

March 18, 1991

ADDRESS REPLY TO
P. O. DRAWER 1734
ATLANTA, GA 30301
———
404 676-3854
FACSIMILE 404 676-7724

Mr. Lazlo Toth
P. O. Box 145
Fairfax, CA 94930

Dear Mr. Toth:

Your recent letter to our late Chairman of the Board, Mr. J. Paul
Austin, about the Coca-Cola machine in the U.S. Embassy in
Kuwait, was forwarded to me for handling. We appreciate your
comments.

Please be advised we were also concerned when that report
appeared on network television. You will be pleased to know that
we did replace the damaged machine with a new one.

Thank you for your interest and we hope you will enjoy receiving
the attached copy of our 1990 annual report.

Sincerely,

Thomas E. Gray

ml

Attachment

P. O. Box 245
Fairfax, California
USA 94930

March 4, 1991

The Emir of Kuwait
Kuwait City, Kuwait

Dear Emir,

I've seen your ads in all the major magazines thanking the American people for our unwavering friendship. On behalf of myself and my friends, you're welcome, and Welcome back to Kuwait!

I saw the news tonight, oh, boy! They reported that during the occupation, when their supply lines were cut off, Iraqi soldiers killed and ate most of the animals in the Kuwait City Zoo. McNeil-Lehrer said they even ate the squirrels! In my opinion, there's nothing worse than for people to come from out of town and eat the animals in someone else's zoo! How low can you go! No manners what so ever!

Everyone else wants to help rebuild your hotels and put out your oil well fires, but who's going to restock your zoo? Who's going to refill those lonely cages? Not the Iraqis! Not the Saudis! Not the Russians! I'll tell you who - The Americans! Once again! Who else!

And so, my Emir, I volunteer! to head the drive to raise money and collect animals to restock Kuwait City Zoo. I will begin with the small animals that are in abundance in my home district - possum, racoon, skunk, woodchucks, rabbits, squirrels, salamanders, etc.

I figure $7500 is about all I'll need from you to start the operation. This should be enough to cover the cost of stationary, office rent and supplies, cages, telephone, feed, shots, newspaper for cages, water bowls, attorney's fees (filing for non-profit tax status), etc.

If it's alright with you, I will call our new joint venture - Unwavering Friendship Enterprises. And besides raising money in America, I will write to the Directors of the Zoos in each of the Coalition Forces Countries to get them to volunteer animals to send to Kuwait.

Send me your picture for the letterhead,

Lazlo Toth

Lazlo Toth
Chief Coordinator, Operation Desert Zoo

87

Unwavering Friendship Enterprises
Operation Desert Zoo

Lazlo Toth
Chief Coordinator

P.O. Box 245
Fairfax, California 94930 USA

To: Zoo Directors of all Coalition Forces Counties
FROM: Lazlo Toth

Dear Fellow Zookeeper,

No doubt you've heard about the zoo atrocities in Kuwait City. Less than one month ago, scores of helpless zoo animals were slaughtered by Iraqi troops in search of meat.

Now is the time to come to the aid of this charred Kingdom. Some are helping by rebuilding hotels, and other choose to fight desert fires - but **you** are in a unique position - Won't you *please* volunteer an animal or two to the Kuwait City Zoo? An elephant, a zebra, a goat? A llama, a panda, the Iraqi's even ate the snakes! Help the Emir and I replenish, restore, and restock! Please inform us what animals you would consider contributing as soon as possible to avoid duplications and feed requirments. All shipping and relocation efforts will be coordinated by our central office in Fairfax, California, USA.

The coalition countries forces stick together - in war, in peace, - and in zoos.

A Zoo without animals is like a tree without a trunk.

Lazlo Toth

Lazlo Toth

3-14-91

World **S**ociety for the **P**rotection of **A**nimals

Sociedad Mundial para la Protección de los Animales

Société Mondiale pour la Protection des Animaux

Welttierschutz-Gesellschaft

WESTERN HEMISPHERE OFFICE   29 PERKINS ST.,   P.O. BOX 190,   BOSTON, MA 02130,   (617) 522-7000   FAX (617) 522-7077

Headquarters
106 Jermyn Street
London SW1Y 6EE
U.K.
Tel: 01-839-3066

Gordon Walwyn, C.V.O.
Director General

Margaret P. Corderoy
F.A.A.I., M.B.I.M.
Group Accountant

Regional Offices
106 Jermyn Street
London SW1Y 6EE
U.K.
Tel: 01-839-3066

Janice H. Cox
European Regional Director

Victor Watkins
Eastern Regional Director

Neil Wells
South Pacific Regional Director
P.O. Box 15-771
New Lynn
Auckland 1232
New Zealand
Tel: 09-878-139

John C. Walsh
Western Regional Director
P.O. Box 190
29 Perkins Street
Boston, MA 02130
U.S.A.
Tel: 617-522-7000

Section Offices
215 Lakeshore Boulevard East
Suite No. 211
Toronto, Ontario M5A 3W9,
Canada
Tel: 416-369-0044

P.O. Box 11733
1001 G S Amsterdam
Netherlands
Tel: 31-20-227-884

Apartado Aereo 75002
Bogota
Colombia
Tel: 571-255-7967

Apartado 516
Heredia
Costa Rica
Tel: 506-397-158

Officers
John A. Hoyt
President

R. Steiner
Hans-Jurgen Weichert
Vice Presidents

Murdaugh S. Madden
Secretary

Robert S. Cummings
Treasurer

Directors
Mme. A. Alessandri, *France*
Mr. E. Bliss, *U.S.A.*
Mr. Robert Cummings,
   U.S.A.
Dr. G. W. Thornton, *U.S.A.*
Mr. F. Dixon Ward, *U.K.*
Mr. G. S. Drysdale, *U.K.*
Mrs. N. Erickson, *Canada*
Mr H P Haering,
   Switzerland
Mrs. Ruth Harrison, *U.K.*
Mr. John Hoyt, *U.S.A.*
Mr. T. Hughes, *Canada*
Mr. Paul Irwin, *U.S.A.*
Mrs. A. Zum Kolk,
   F.R. Germany
Prof. Dr. H. Kraft,
   F.R. Germany
Mrs. E. Lagerstrom,
   Sweden
Mrs. Yvonne Lando,
   Belgium
Herr G. von Langheim,
   Austria
Mrs. K. Longman, *U.K.*
Mrs. F. McAllister, *Ireland*
Dr. M. S. Madden, *U.S.A.*
Mons. J. Maury, *France*
Dr. T. Metveit, *Norway*
Mr. Otto Ratz, *Hungary*
Mr. A. Richmond, *U.K.*
Sir Cameron Rusby, *U.K.*
Mr. T. H. Scott, *U.K.*
Mrs. A. Singh, *India*
Mr. Arthur Slade, *U.S.A.*
Mr. R. Steiner, *Switzerland*
Mr. D. Vescovo, *Italy*
Dr. Hans-Jurgen Weichert,
   F.R. Germany
Mr. D. Wills, *U.S.A.*
Mr. W. Wiseman, *U.S.A.*
Herr Arno J.H. Zuang,
   Luxembourg
Mr. A. Zwanenburg,
   Netherlands

April 3, 1991

Lazlo Toth
Chief Coordinator
Unwavering Friendship Enterprises
P.O. Box 245
Fairfax, CA 94930

Dear Mr. Toth:

The World Society for the Protection of Animals (WSPA)
is an international organization engaged in animal welfare
and rescue projects throughout the world. WSPA, through
the leadership of International Projects Director John
Walsh, is coordinating all animal relief and rescue efforts
in Kuwait.

WSPA recently became aware of your efforts to acquire
zoo animals to ship to the Kuwait Zoo in order to replenish
the stock. While your sentiments are appreciated, WSPA
is strongly opposed to this plan.

The Kuwait Zoo, where Mr. Walsh is overseeing operations,
has been badly damaged and is not in a position to reopen. Even if restored to its original state, the zoo
would not meet minimal standards that would allow it to
operate in the United States.

The cages are cold, damp, dark, cramped and without room
for the animals to exercise. The living conditions in
no way resemble the animals' natural habitat.
Additionally, the animals that have survived to this point
face a shortage of food and water. Mr. Walsh's opinion
is that the zoo in its present configuration should never
be re-opened.

Plans to construct a new zoo in Kuwait have been designed
but the realization of these plans is several years away.
Any efforts to send animals to Kuwait presently are mis-
guided and inappropriate.

Should you wish to contribute to the animal relief efforts in Kuwait,
we encourage you to contact our Boston office directly at (617) 522-
7000. We can then work together through the direction of WSPA
personnel in Kuwait to best conduct these activities.

Thank you very much.

Sincerely,

Nick W. Manzella
Field Officer

P.O. Box 245
Fairfax, California 94930
March 19, 1991! St. Joseph's Day!

Mr. Perry Kinney
Kinney Shoes Corporation
6600 Topanga Canyon SP 97E
Canoga Park, Calif. 91303

Dear Mr. Kinney,

It sure wasn't easy to track you down! Do you know that most people that work in your store on the Miracle Mile don't even know that they're part of a national chain? They seemed quite upset when I told them. Up till now they thought they were the only one! I was forced to call an 800 customer service number to get your address! But, at least you're listed, that's more than I can say for some people (McDonald's).

Mr. Kinney, I could send this idea to Nike or Thom McAnn or some sock company, but I chose you because I know how to return a favor. A while back I had some financial misunderstandings with the McDonald's Corporation, and one of your employees was kind enough to try to help me resolve it. It's a long story, but to make it short, it <u>was</u> resolved, and now on to more important things:

Mr. Kinney!, I have an idea for a commercial campaign for you. It's based on <u>THE WIND BENEATH MY WINGS</u> by the singer Betty Midler. Hers is about a person, but mine is about two particular parts of a person - the feet. Since the feet are also the most important part of a human in your particular business, I'm giving you first crack at my idea:

<u>Saluting Feet (Advertising Campaign) by Lazlo Toth</u>
1. The film/visual part is all close up shots of feet:
Show bare feet running on the beach, climbing stairs, walking in the desert, etc., and then you switch to shots of feet slipping into Kinney shoes. Then you see the whole person who's feet it is and it turns out to be a famous person, like Cher, or General Schwarzkopt.
2. Here is a sample of <u>The Lyrics</u>:

<u>The feet within my shoes</u>
Did I ever tell you're my hero's
Tho' you're the farthest parts of me
I can run faster than a Beagle
You are the feet beneath my knees.

I'll send you the second verse
after we sign the contracts,

Lazlo Toth

Lazlo Toth

KINNEY SHOE CORPORATION
6600 TOPANGA CANYON BLVD.
SPACE 97-E
CANOGA PARK, CA 91303
818-594-4916

PERRY KINNEY
REGIONAL VICE PRESIDENT
PACIFIC REGION

April 4, 1991

Mr. Lazlo Toth
P.O. Box 245
Fairfax, CA 94930

Dear Mr. Toth:

Thank you for sending your proposal for an advertising campaign
for the Kinney Shoe Corporation.

I have forwarded your proposal to our Advertising Department and
if they are interested in your idea, they will contact you.

Sincerely,

Perry Kinney

PK:ls

Post Office Box 245
Fairfax, California 94930
March 22, 1991

Mr. Ed Rensi, President
McDonald's Hamburgers World Headquarters
Oak Brook, Illinois 60521

Dear Mr. Rensi,
 Congradulations!
 Your new, low fat McLean Deluxe burger that I just read about on the
FRONT PAGE of the this morning's <u>Chronicle,</u> is a fine idea for the 90's and I
hope it will help "counter sluggish sales", although my Mac place doesn't
have that problem - it's always full! Maybe if they weren't so busy they'd
give out french fries with a Fish sandwich instead of too many napkins in a
McRib Pack bag, and I didn't even order ribs! Anyway, that's water over
the bridge.
 Here's the reason why I'm writing now: I have an idea for a burger that
will <u>really</u> help counter sluggish sales! Way better than the McLean Deluxe!
Mr. Rensi, I introduce you to - <u>Little Big Mac!</u>

The boss takes a bite: *McDonald's president Ed Rensi*

<u>Little Big Mac</u>
Half the Fat with a *feather* on top!

 The feather I pasted in the photo is much bigger than those we will use on
the the top of our L.B.M. We will use the same great ingredients as the
famous Big Mac, but! in <u>miniature</u> (half the meat=half the fat), <u>and,</u> with an
Indian motif (free feather). Dennis Kostner recently won the Academy
Award Oscar for the film, <u>Dances with Wolves,</u> and it also had an Indian
motif! Perhaps we can get him for the campaign.
Also, I'm thinking of putting Dustin Hoffman in it.

  Awaiting your reply - let's not dilly dally on this one!

Lazlo Toth

Lazlo Toth

McDonald's Corporation
McDonald's Plaza
Oak Brook, Illinois 60521
Direct Dial Number

(708) 575-6198

May 1, 1991

Mr. Lazlo Toth
P. O. Box 245
Fairfax, CA 94930

Dear Mr. Toth:

Thank you for your interest in McDonald's and for taking the time to write.

We have tested a "mini" version of the Big Mac. This sandwich contained one
hamburger patty, a single bun, low calorie cheese, and low calorie Big Mac
sauce. While we have no plans to add it to our regular menu at this time,
perhaps you'll see a smaller version of the Big Mac some day at your local
McDonald's.

Again, thank you for writing McDonald's. Please use the enclosed gift
certificates the next time you visit McDonald's. We look forward to serving
you for many years to come.

Sincerely,

McDONALD'S CORPORATION

Shari Petty

Shari R. Petty
Representative
Customer and Community Relations

Gift Certificate BD 386023

Gift Certificate BD 386024

To:

From: See reverse side for details.

Proud Sponsor
of the 1992
U.S. Olympic Team

USA

Give the great tastes of McDonald's
any time of the year.

90¢

URGENT

L. Toth
P. O. Box 245
Fairfax, California
94930 USA

Fairfax, March 23, 1991

Archbishop Traian Crisan
S e c r e t a r y
Congregation for the Causes of the Saints
Vatican City,
Vatican (State)

Your Eminence,

I know the church moves slow, but it's five months since I wrote to you regarding the Fr. **Junipero Serra** miracle - and not a word from Rome!

I'm trying to arrange my schedule for the next few months and if the canonical investigating team is coming I'd like at least a few weeks notice.

I just don't understand why things are moving so slowly. It will be three years in September since Father Serra appeared to me and gave me the idea for the gum. Over five years ago, he cured a nun of lupus, you know that! That was a miracle, and now this! Let's get going! I'm not blaming your staff, I like my naps and spaghetti, too, but there's a time and a place for everything, and now is the time for Father **Junipero Serra** sainthood! This cause may not seem urgent to them, but we want him named Saint now before those Indian beater charges spread.

The egg will not go back into the shell!

Lazlo Toth

Lazlo Toth

Fr. Junipero Serra Prayer Group
The egg will not go back into the shell!

P.O. Box 245 / Fairfax, California/ 94930

April 26, 1991

Director
Nixon Library and Birthplace
Yorba Linda, California

Dear Director:

My prayer group is planning a trip to the Father Junipero Serra statue on Route 280, and some of us will be continuing on to Southern California to visit Disneyland and the Nixon Library.

At present our schedule has us arriving at the Library on May 28th, at 7:30 a.m., and we would like to know if your cafeteria will be open at that hour.

Lazlo Toth

Lazlo Toth

NO REPLY !

P.O. Box 245
Fairfax, California 94930
May 25, 1991

Shari R. Petty
Representative of Relations
McDonald's Corporation
Oak Brook, Illinois 60521

Dear Ms. Petty,

I see what you're trying to do, you're not fooling anybody!, and the sad fact is that you don't know a good idea when you read one! To infer that my "Little Big Mac" is the same as your "mini" version of the Big Mac infers to me that you don't even know what a Big Mac is! No wonder why you've got sluggish sales! And it's no wonder that your "Mini" low calorie McWimp creation was a flop in the test market! You called it a "mini" Big Mac and it wasn't! You misrepresented the name of the greatest sandwich in America! Didn't you learn anything from Coca-Cola? Are we going to see "Big Mac Classic" next? My idea is like putting Coca-Cola in smaller bottles, not changing the formula!

My "Little Big Mac" is the EXACT same thing as a Big Mac, -only smaller! That's why I call it "Litttle" Big Mac. I can't believe you don't see the difference! Also you don't seem to appreciate the value and great marketing possibilities of the Indian motif! Try putting a feather on top of your "mini" Big Mac and people will laugh at you! It just wouldn't go! And do you think Dustin Hoffman would want to get involved with a "Mini" Big Mac? He wouldn't touch it with a ten foot poll!, and who could blame him - it has absolutly NOTHING to do with Indians!

I guess Mr. Rensi was traveling so you somehow got a hold of my letter to him. I know that if he read it personally he would agree with me that your "mini version" is not the same thing as my "Little Big Mac".

Also it did not go unnoticed by me that you sent me back my original letter to Mr. Rensi! I wonder why you did that and hope that you will reconsider telling Mr. Rensi about my idea.

Also, thanks for the gift certificates, but I don't think it would be wise for me to accept them at this time.

Lazlo Toth

Lazlo Toth

June 6, 1991
Post Office Box 245, Fairfax, California 94930

The Richard Nixon Library & Birthplace
18001 Yorba Linda Boulevard
Yorba, Linda, Calfornia USA 92686

Dear Director,

    As you must imagine, it was quite a disappointment to discover that
RNL&B does not only not serve breakfast, but you don't even have a
cafeteria! You call it "Southern California's Newest Family Attraction", and
there's not even any food! Whoever heard of a Family Attraction without
food! I don't know who the architect was, but somebody got taken to the
cleaners!

    My group and I were all set to eat breakfast when we arrived there at
7:20 am on Friday of Memorial Day Weekend. I told them I couldn't promise
the cafeteria would be open that early, but most of us took the chance and
waited to have our breakfast at the L&B instead of at Disneyland before we
left. As you can imagine, I had some disgruntled prayer group partners on
my hands when they found out that not only do you not have a cafeteria, but
that you didn't even have the manners to write us back to let us know you
didn't have one. Is a little common courtesy to much to ask from a
Presidential library? Let me answer that question myself: Evidently, yes!

    However!, I was quite impressed by the Life Size Statues of the Famous
World Leaders, and maybe it was because I was so hungry, but I couldn't
help thinking, "I wonder if Winston Churchill and President Nixon ate
breakfast before their meeting?" And then I thought, "I wonder what they
ate after their meeting?" And that's how I came up with the idea for-

President Richard M. Nixon Historical Microwavable T.V. Dinners

Enclosed is a preliminary packaging design for my first frozen recreation:
The President Nixon /Chairman Mao TV Banquet.

    I know President Nixon is public domain, but I have no idea how the
Chinese handle something like this. Should some of the proceeds go to the
Tse Tung estate, or should I send it directly to the communist party?
I'm sure the Nixon organization still has many contacts in Peking. Please
help me by passing this along through the proper channels in China so I can
obtain the necessary releases and recipes.

                        Lazlo Toth

P.O. Box 245
Fairfax, California 94930

July 5, 1991

Hon. John Sunnunu
Chief of Staff
The White House
Washington, D.C.

Dear Chief,

Well, I see the turkey buzzard press is coming down on you again. You try to do good and go by limo to New York so you can stay in constant contact with the White House, and they jump on you like you traveled there in an armored convoy.
If I were you, I'd tell them, "I'm the Chief-of-Staff, I could have gone to the rare stamp auction by Fire Truck if I wanted to! And a Hook and Ladder takes <u>two</u> drivers - not just one! You need a driver in the back <u>and</u> the front, -so back off!"

One does not have to be a member of the Mega society to know that they're picking on you because of your Eskimo ancestry. Hang in there! And remember, even if the worst should happen, you can always write a book: <u>Appearance of Impropriety</u> by John Sunnunu. That would be worth a million, -or more!

I am sending you a stamp from my personal collection. It's from back when it only cost twenty-five cents to mail a letter - April! And I hear they haven't printed Christmas stamps yet because they're thinking of raising the price AGAIN! If you could put a stop to rising postal rates, you could overcome your Big Spender image, and become a hero to all the people who are sick of always paying more and more for postage that takes longer and longer to get to people who don't even answer you half the time.

Looking forward to your help in this matter,

Lazlo Toth

Lazlo Toth

THE WHITE HOUSE

WASHINGTON

September 12, 1991

Dear Mr. Toth,

Thank you for your letter and kind words. I
appreciate your taking the time to write.

Sincerely,

John H. Sununu
Chief of Staff

Mr. Lazlo Toth
Post Office Box 245
Fairfax, California 94930

P.O. Box 245
Fairfax, California
94930
July 15, 1991

Mr. Ed Rensi, President
McDonald's Hamburger Corporation
McDonald's World Headquarters Plaza
Oak Brook, Illinois 60521

Dear Ed,

    As I'm sure you're well aware, 1992 marks the 20th anniversary of the introduction of the Filet-O-Fish Sandwich, and I was wondering if you had anything planned yet for the celebration or if I should start working something up.

    I'm thinking of a Chrisopher Columbus angle, tying in the celebration of the 500th aniversay of the discovery of America with the invention of the Filet-O-Fish.

Regards to everyone in Oak Brook,

Lazlo Toth

Lazlo Toth

P.S.

Still waiting to hear from you regarding the "Little Big Mac" business.
I figure if we have a deal, I might approach Dustin Hoffman on both projects.
I just hope some people won't be offended if he plays Columbus in one and an Indian in the other. One way to go would be for him to play an Indian in both - maybe he's the one who gives Columbus a Filet-O-Fish right after he lands. Anyway, that's down the road.

FROM YOUR FRIEND

Ronald McDonald ®

September 19, 1991

Mr. Lazlo Toth
P.O. Box 245
Fairfax, California 94930

Dear Lazlo,

    Good to hear from you after all these years. Are you
still putting jelly on the top half of your hamburger
buns?

    Listen, Lazlo, hold off on that promotion of Filet-O-
Fish and Christopher Columbus -- your research department
misled you. McDonald's introduced the Filet-O-Fish in
1963, so 1992 will be our 29-year anniversary. Not quite
the zip of a 20th anniversary, is it?

    Maybe you could develop something with an Italian
flavor -- after all, we're testing pizza and a number of
pasta dishes in our restaurants right now. But, drop the
Dustin Hoffman angle -- we need someone right "off the
boat"...like Father Guido Sarducci, if he's available.
Maybe you could ask. (He's on Johnny Carson a lot, but
he might be retiring when Johnny does, like Ed McMahon.
I don't know how show business works.)

    Support your local McDonald's!

                              Your friend,

                              Ronald McDonald

cc: Ed Rensi, president and CEO, McDonald's USA

NO REPLY !

DEFICIT BEER

D$

A beer for the greater good
that's really good!

P.O. Box 245
Fairfax, California
USA 94930
July 4, 1991 -10 P.M. PST

August A. Busch III
Anheuser-Busch Companies
One Busch Plaza
St. Louis, MO. USA 63118-1852

Dear Mr. Busch,

It's a little late and I'm tired, but I've decided to write while the spirit moves me. The 4th of July is already yesterday in St. Louis, but it's still here for two more hours, so Happy 4th of July, even though it's over for you - it's still happening here! That's the advantage of living on the west coast!

This afternoon, I was sharing a beer with my friend, George Tuttle, when he asked me,"Whatever happened to your idea for PRESIDENT BUSH "kinder, gentler" BEER?" I told him how we got stuck in kind of a power struggle, and how neither of us were willing to budge on the two and a half cents per six pack issue. Tuttle is kind of a philosopher type, and he said I should offer it up and bend a little because of the benefit to society because of the paying off the deficit part.

I looked inside myself. I searched my soul. I thought about "the greater good". And, so, Mr. Busch, you can tell your legal people that I am willing to reopen negotiations and reconsider the two and half cents issue.
But, since the "kinder, gentler" angle seems a little old, and also doesn't seem to apply because of recent world events (Iraq War), I would like to drop that advertising theme entirely and concentrate instead on the paying off the deficit part.
Also, I would like to change the name from "PRESIDENT BUSH BEER" to "DEFICIT BEER", and have two and a half cents (or more) from every six pack go to help pay off the national debt. The debt is getting worse, day by day, and everybody likes beer - this could be the solution America is looking for! Together, you and I, with the help of millions of beer drinkers, can wipe out the national debt - once and for all!

There's "Good" Beer and there's "Great" Beer,
But there's only one beer that's good for the "Greater Good"!
DEFICIT BEER! A Great Beer, that's really Good!

Lazlo Toth *Lazlo Toth*

P.O. Box 245
Fairfax, California 94930
August 15, 1991

President
Swanson Foods
Campbell Soup Company
Camden, N.J. USA 08103-1701

Dear Sir:

I have enjoyed your Hungry-Man Dinners for some time now and enjoy the turkey dinner especially. The stuffing is excellent.

Not long ago, I visited the Richard Nixon Library and Birthplace in Yorba Linda, California. The place has some architectual flaws, but all in all, it's a fine monument to a great President. It was at the RNL&B that I got the idea of recreating historic meals from Presdient Nixon's life - frozen microwavable recreations of his state dinners with world leaders like deGaulle, Khrushchev, Mao, Gandhi, etc. Plus meals from special occasions in his life: Everyone saw his famous Watergate resignation speech, but how many people know what he ate before the speech? Answer: His favorite dish, Chicken with Cauliflower, also known as the fancy name, Chicken Divan.

I thought it would be a good idea if the RNL&B would serve these meals in their cafeteria, but, you won't belive this - they don't even have one! Then I thought perhaps they could sell the meals there and people could microwave them at home. But now I have a bigger idea. I plan to expand my President Nixon Historical Microwavable TV Dinner idea to other Presidents!

I am now actively in the process of looking for a partner with experience in the frozen dinner field.   At present I have packaging samples for 24 of the 40 Presidents. I have inclosed samples for Jimmy Carter (#38), and Gerald Ford (#37), and I am currently working on Martin Van Buren (#8) and Grover Cleveland (#22), which will bring the total to 26.

You could add these dinners to the Hungry-Man line and call them "Hungry-President Dinners", but I would prefer calling them "Fit for a President Microwave Dinners" and use the Presidential Seal as our logo.

I have tested all meals myself and they are delicious,

Lazlo Toth

Lazlo Toth

Campbell Soup Company

September 4, 1991

Mr. Lazlo Toth
P. O. Box 245
Fairfax, CA 94930

Dear Mr. Toth,

Thank you for your letter and suggestion. It is especially nice to hear from people such as you who have an interest in our work and our products.

While we appreciate your good intentions, it is our policy to advise you and other consumers who submit interesting ideas about our predicament. Very often the suggestions offered to us are similar to those developed by our own staff and are already underway. In other cases, we may not have a current business need for a particular idea.

If we receive a suggestion that coincides with an idea we are already considering and we proceed with our idea, then the letter writer may think that we appropriated his or her idea. To avoid any such awkward situations and misunderstandings, we have found it best to rely on our own staff.

Please accept our sincere thanks, however, for taking the time to write to us. We take great pride in the quality of our products and it's rewarding to know that you share our dedication.

Sincerely,

Florence Boskey

Florence Boskey
Consumer Correspondent

NO REPLY !

P. O. Box 245
Fairfax, California
94930 USA
August 23, 1991

President Mikhail Gorbachev
The Kremlin
Moscow, Russia
USSR

Dear Mr. President,

Welcome back! We were all quite worried about you when they announced there was a Coup. Especially when Vice President Gennady Yanayev, the new "acting President", said you were "sick". But nobody believed that line except the <u>Washington Post</u>, and that's probably because they have CIA guys who are really KGB guys working there. Next thing you know they'll be telling us Deep Throat was Sammy Davis Jr.!

I think it was right after it came out that Gennady was known as "the Russian Dan Quale" that the news media people started saying the coup wasn't going to make it. They're saying that the coup failed, but it looks to me like Boris Yeltsin was the coup! I'm not saying he planned the whole thing with former President Reagan last year at a secret meeting at the Mayo Clinic, when they both pretended to be patients there, or that Reagan's friends from the Hoover Institute had anyting to do with it, - all I know is that it's a week later and Russia is being run by Yeltsin and a bunch of advisers from Stanford! You don't have to be a blood relative of William Casey's to know a coup when you see one, even if it's not the one that they wanted us to see. And even though Yeltsin may be the new boy on the block in the USSR, you are still America's favorite Russian! All the toy stores are reporting that your dolls are really selling well!

Mr. President!, I am working on a line of "Fit for a President" (of the United States) frozen TV dinners, and if it's as successful as I think it's going to be, we will eventually be expanding to Presidents of other countries. If you don't mind me asking, would you please let me know what you ate for your first meal after you returned to power?

To me, Yeltsin always looks like man who just had his accordian stolen. (You can use that),

Lazlo Toth

Lazlo Toth

P.O. Box 245
Fairfax, California 94930

9-1-91

Director
Graceland
Memphis, Tennessee

Dear Director,

   I know Graceland is not for sale, but if it was, what do you think the
asking price would be?   This is not an offer, it is merely an inquiry.
I know real estate in Memphis isn't very expensive compared to most other
areas in the Nation, but I also know Graceland is a unique property and
worth a lot more than similar sized homes in the area.

   Also, I would like to know where I can purchase the photograph of Elvis
shaking hands with President Nixon. I think it was taken the day that
President Nixon made Elvis a secret agent.

   The last time I was at Graceland was in '78, when Elvis' Uncle Fester was
still working the gate! I'll bet there have been a lot of improvements to the
property since then.

          Thanking you in advance,

          Lazlo Toth

          Lazlo Toth

December 30, 1991

Lazlo Toth
P.O. Box 245
Fairfax, CA 94930

Dear Lazlo:

This is in response to your letter dated September 1, 1991, concerning
Graceland Mansion.

First of all, I apologize for the delay in responding to your letter. The delay is
simply due to a tremendous amount of mail that we receive on a daily basis and
it takes awhile to answer it all.

In response to your question concerning how much Graceland might be worth,
should it be for sale. Well - first, Graceland is not for sale, and it would be hard
to even begin estimating how much the asking price would be set at.

In your letter, you asked where you might obtain photographs of Elvis and
President Nixon. You may write to the National Archives at the address listed in
the information I have enclosed for you.

Again, I am sorry for the delay in responding to your letter, and we greatly
appreciate your interest in Elvis and Graceland.

Sincerely,

Paige Cline
Administrative Assistant
Communications Department
GRACELAND, DIVISION OF
ELVIS PRESLEY ENTERPRISES, INC.

/ptc

P.O. Box 245 - Fairfax, California - 94930

9-1-91

President Adele Simmons
John D. and Catherine T. MacArthur Foundation
140 S. Dearborn
Chicago, Illinois 60607

Dear President Simmons,

I saw an article about your organization in a magazine at the library, and hope you and the MacArthur's will be able to help me in a most important endeaver.

I understand your Foundation awards $140 million annually for "genius grants" and "worthy projects". Ms. Simmons, I'm no genius, but I have a worthy project!

Ms. Simmons, I have a Plan for Peace in the Middle East!

At this time, I'm still working on the budget, and I'm not sure what my Peace Plan will cost. I don't think I'll need the whole $140 million, but it will be expensive because my plan involves compensating and relocating a very V.I.P., his family, his servants, and his staff. If your organization has some kind of a trade off deal with an airline it will sure help.

Please send me your application forms as soon as possible.

Together, we can do what statesmen and politicians have been trying to do since 1948 - bring peace and harmony to The Middle East, one of the most volatile regions in the world as we know it today.

Pacem in Terris (Peace on Earth in Latin),

Lazlo Toth

140 South Dearborn Street   Chicago, Illinois 60603-5285
Suite 1100   Telephone: (312) 726-8000

THE JOHN D. AND CATHERINE T.

MacArthur Foundation

September 23, 1991

Mr. Lazio Toth
P.O. Box 245
Fairfax, CA 94930

Dear Mr. Toth:

We are responding to your request for information about grant opportunities for individuals by sending brochures describing the selection process for the MacArthur Fellows Program and the Program on Peace and International Cooperation's Research and Writing competition. I am sorry to report that the MacArthur Foundation is prohibited from rendering support to individuals except through two clearly defined programs that have the approval of the Internal Revenue Service.

The Program on Peace and International Cooperation makes grants to individuals based on the results of an annual competition open to scholars exploring issues in international relations. Awards are restricted to winners of the Peace Program's annual Research and Writing competition. The MacArthur Fellows Program also makes awards to individuals, but only those who have been nominated and selected through its carefully defined nominating process. Self nominations, informal nominations, and nominations originating outside the program's nominating structure are not accepted.

I hope the enclosed brochures and this letter explain why it is impossible for the MacArthur Foundation to render financial support to individuals in most cases. We do, however, wish you success in finding financial support for your project.

Sincerely,

Richard J. Kaplan
Director of Grants Management,
Research and Information

RJK/dtl

Enclosures

Lazlo Toth
P.O. Box 245
Fairfax, California
94930 U.S.A.

Florence Boskey
Consumer Correspondent
Campbell Soup Company
Camden, N.J. 08103-1701

9-12-91

NO REPLY !

Dear Consumer Correspondent Boskey,

   I was quite surprised to receive a letter from the Campbell Soup Company regarding my "Fit for a President Microwave Dinners", since I sent my proposal and packaging samples to the Swanson (T.V. Dinner) Company, not Campbell's Soup. Afterall, your company makes soup, not frozen dinners, everybody knows that.

   The only reason I put "Campbell Soup Company" on my letter to Swanson's was because it say's on the back of the <u>Swanson Hungy Man Turkey (mostly white meat) Dinner</u>, "Write: Swanson Food, Campbell Soup Company, Camden N.J."

   Clearly, my letter was to Swanson's, and I just don't understand why you Campbell's Soup people opened it in the first place. And then, when you saw that my idea was for Frozen (Historical) Dinners, and had absolutely nothing to do with soup, instead of acknowledging your mistake and forwarding it to Swansons, (frozen Tv dinner specialists!), you send me a letter saying my idea (Fit For A President Microwavable Dinners), is "similar" to an idea already developed by your staff. How can this be when my idea has to do with Microwavable Historical Dinners and your company makes soup!

   I can only conclude from your letter that Campbells is blatantly cutting Swanson out of the deal, and is secretly preparing to go head to head with me in the Frozen Presidential T.V. Dinner field. And one does not have to be born in Vienna to figure out that your discouraging letter and free soup coupons are merely diversions to trick me into abandoning my frozen brain child, and steer my creative juices away from this untapped, lucrative arena.

   Ms. Boskey, where has all this back biting and clandestine manuvering led us? Has it helped either of us? I'll answer that question myself - No! It's clear that if we want to crack this market, cooperation is the key!

   Although I have been thrown by Campbell's hostile buiness methods, I have not stopped cooking. I am happy to report that I have now completed frozen entres for all 41 Presidents, and in the spirit of coorperation, I have added small portions of Soup to the dinners of all the Presidents who served more than one term. Cream of Mushroom for the Democrats and Cream of Celery for the Republicans. Also, I thought you might like to know, our Warren Harding Poker Party Dinner will be the first microwave dinner in History to include pretzels!

                    Let's face it, we need each other!

                         Lazlo Toth

P.O. Box 245   Fairfax, California   94930
September 13, 1991

Vice President Dan Quale
Vice President of the United States
The Mansion of the Vice President
Washington, District of Columbia

Dear Vice President Quale,

Congradulations are in order for the fine way you represented us in Malawi. Welcome back, you are back now!

All we usually hear about you are negative stories, and it's nice to hear how smoothly your talks went with President Banda. He's getting on in years, and I hope you didn't come down on him too hard for not letting people vote. Afterall, people didn't get to vote for you either. Not directly, anyway. If people had a choice, and could vote for President and Vice-President separately, we might have seen President Banda sitting next to Vice-President Benson last week, instead of you, - if you get my drift.

Change the subject. I heard a story that you were asked what you were going to do to counter all the negative feelings people have regarding your ability to be President, if that day (God forbid) should ever come, and you said, "I have but one word to say about that, - 'try harder'." Mr. Vice President, is this story true? You don't have to write me a long letter about it, just say one word - "Yes", or, "No".

I know that if you had to, you could fly the plane!

Lazlo Toth

Laz...

Post Office Box 245
Fairfax, California
U.S.A.   94930

Friday, September 13, 1991

Life President Hastings Kamuzu Banda
Blantyre, Malawi

Dear Life President Banda,

Many thanks for giving such a warm welcome to our Vice President, Dan Quale, during his recent trip to your country.

All we usually hear about Malawi are the stories about human rights abuses and how you always put your political opponents in jail, and it's nice to hear how well you and our V.P. hit it off.

Please send me a picture of yourself with V.P. Quale.

Don't ever step aside,

Lazlo Toth

Lazlo Toth

P.S.
I know you haven't had an election there since 1950, but if you still happen to have one of your old campaign buttons around, I'd love one for my collection.

P. O. Box 245
Fairfax, California
94930
September 15, 1991

President
United Airlines
P.O. Box 66100
Chicago, Illinois
60666

Dear Sir:

i have but one question: Why is the food so bad?

Everyone wants to know - not just me,

Lazlo Toth

Lazlo Toth

UNITED AIRLINES

Executive Offices

October 15, 1991

Mr. Lazlo Toth
P.O. Box 245
Fairfax, CA 94930

Dear Mr. Toth:

Thank you for writing. We regret the disappointment you experienced
with our meal service. Please accept our apology.

Of the millions of meals we prepare each year, the vast majority are
well prepared and meet our customers' expectations. Despite our best
efforts, a problem will occur now and then and we do follow up with our
Food Service management when disservice is brought to our attention.

We appreciate your comments, and we will share them with our Food
Service department.

Sincerely,

Lillian R. Lofton

Lillian R. Lofton
Customer Relations

REF #: 0587817A

LRL/cl

Box 245 Fairfax, California 94930

9-19-1991

Prime Minister Valeriu Muravski
Republic of Moldavia
Kishinev, Moldavia

Dear Prime Minister Muravski,

On behalf of all the American people, Congradulations! and Welcome
Aboard! I know it's not easy to start a new country, especially in the midst
of a recession, and you must have a "Things To Do List" a kilometer long.
Well, you can scratch "New National Anthem" off your list, because I've
taken care of that for you!

Although I am not of Moldavian descent, and have never had the pleasure
of traveling to your neck of the woods, I think I make up for those facts with
my extensive songwriting background. My experience includes "Political
Fight Songs", and "pick me upper" tunes, mostly written for Former President
Richard M. Nixon. And on the International front, I have written tunes for
the Queen of England (Elizabeth Windsor), and Emperor Bokassa I.

By concentrating in the lyrics arena, I have had the chance to collaborate
with some of the finest composers of the 20th Century (as well as the 19th).
For the Moldavian National Anthem, I have set my words to a stirring
melody by one of America's most gifted composers - Mr. Neil Diamonds.
The great thing about all of Mr. Diamonds' songs are that they make you
want to march, and matched with appropriate lyrics they make perfect
anthems and are tailor made for Olympic events, as well as for half time use.
I don't know if you have half time over there yet, but the way things are
going, it won't be long.

No down payment is necessary at present, but my fees generally run
between $50 and $70 for lyrics for a project like this, plus I will want to be
paid a small amount everytime the song is played or hummed at sporting
events, swearing in ceremonies, television sign offs, etc.

Mr. Prime Minister, enclosed please find Moldavia's new National Anthem,
<u>I AM MOLDAVIA, I SAID.</u>   I would include a cassette of me singing it, but I
don't know what kind of volts you have.

Lazlo Toth

Lazlo Toth

I Am Moldavia...I Said
(L. Toth - N. Diamonds)

Moscow's not fine, when you want to dine, you stand in line,
three hours in Red Square for a Big Mac!
Standing in snow, the line is slow, and you know,
all I can think about is makin' my way back.

Well I'm Moldavian born and bred
and since the Coup I'm no longer torn between two Republics..
Moscow's fine, if you like standing in lines
Sure!, Moldavia's got lines, but at least the lines are mine!

I am MOLDAVIA, I said,
I am MOLDAVIA, said I!
MOLDAVIA! I said
MOLDAVIA! Said I!

I am MOLDAVIA, I said
I am MOLDAVIA, said I!
I said MOLDAVIA !
MOLDAVIA! said I!

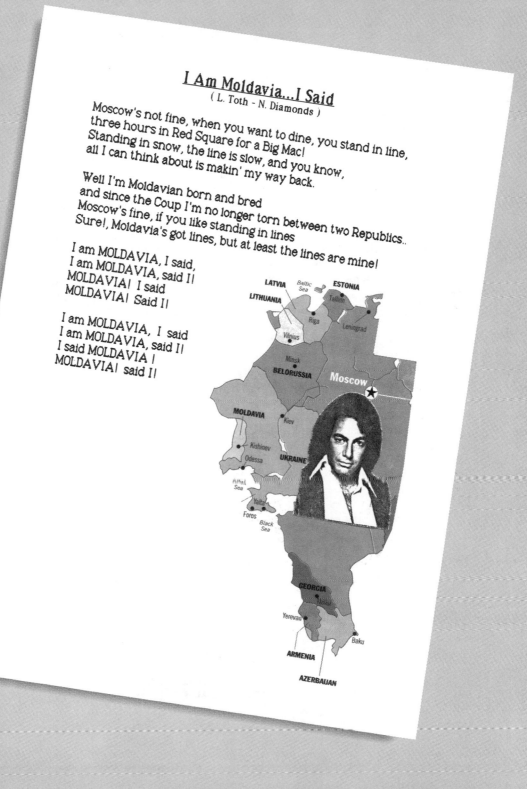

117

9-19-1991

Broadcast Music International
320 West 57th Street
New York, New York 10019

Dear BMI:

   I am in the process of writing National Anthems for each of the new
breakaway republics in what was formerlly known as the USSR, and I need
your help. I think it is important that all the songs in this historic
confederation of anthems be similar, yet somewhat different, and so, I have
decided to put my lyrics to melodies written by the singer Neil Diamonds.

   I have written my lyrics in English and will entrust their translation to
local authorities, but I will insist to each of the republics that Mr. Diamonds'
melodies remain relatively intact.

   I am concerned that perhaps I may need Mr. Diamonds' approval for this
transSoviet musical endeavor. I wouldn't want Diamonds suing Lithuania or
some other struggling republic on my account! That's all they need! It's
expensive to start new countries now days! The start up costs are
staggering - new flag, new stationary, new Pledge of Allegience, etc. - and
they sure don't need the added cost of defending themselves in an
international court of law just because their national anthem sounds just like
Cracklin' Rosie or one of his other tunes!

   Please tell Mr. Diamonds that I am not inexperienced in the song writing
field. I have adapted many songs for Former President Richard M. Nixon
(Best!), among others, and have co-written with such well known composers
as Cole Porter, Steven Foster, and Betty Midler. However, this is the first
time I will graft my words to more than one melody by any one single
individual.

   Specifically, the songs I have co-written with Mr. Diamonds are:

        I Am I Said (Moldavia)
        Song Sung Blue (Lithuania)
        Sweet Caroline (Estonia)
        Cherry, Cherry (Azerbaijan)
        Thank the Lord for the Night Time (Latvia)
        Brother Love's Traveling Salvation Show (Uzbekistan)

        Vigortz and Soolaimon!

        Lazlo Toth   Lazlo Toth

March 26, 1992

Mr. Lazlo Toth
Box 245
Fairfax, CA 94930

Dear Mr. Toth:

Your letter to BMI of September 19th, was recently forwarded to my attention. I would like to apologize for the unusual amount of time it took to reply to this letter. Work here came to a virtual standstill some time ago as the result of some sort of contest involving pizzas and popes. Needless to say, this caused quite a backlog in our correspondence.

I wish that I could be of more help to you in your quest to secure permission to create national anthems for the emerging European nations. It would warm my heart to know that, as these plucky people struggle to forge a new world for themselves, as they merrily go off to work each day whistling the joyous anthems you made for them, that I had some part, however small, in assisting you in your noble task.

As I say, I wish I could assist you but I cannot. Mr. Neil Diamonds' music is, to the best of my knowledge, licensed through ASCAP. I would suggest that you contact them at 1 Lincoln Plaza, New York, NY 10022. They may be able to provide you with publisher information for your future anthems.

Please contact me if I may be of further assistance.

Sincerely,

Paul Casciani
Research & Information

320 West 57th Street, New York, New York 10019-3790   (212) 586-2000   Telex: 127823

To Our Catalog Buyers:

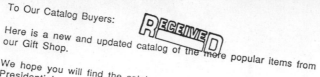

Here is a new and updated catalog of the more popular items from our Gift Shop.

We hope you will find the catalog a welcome resource for unique Presidential specialties for yourself, family, friends, business associates and everyone you know who is interested in the Nixon years, the Presidency, and the Nixon Presidential Museum.

There is a handy order form on the last page.

With the holidays not far off, we thought you would want to know what is available and place orders early. Please note that we offer several unique ornaments, and a great collection of gift ideas.

Write, fax or call us if your have any questions (see page 6 for our phone and fax numbers). Enjoy reading about the diversity of our collection, and we hope to hear from you soon.

Sincerely

Carolyn Hawley

Carolyn Hawley
Gift Shop Manager

THE RICHARD NIXON · LIBRARY & BIRTHPLACE

1991 GIFT CATALOG

Featuring an outstanding collection of books, sportswear, art work, accessories, souvenirs, original specialties and Grand Opening momentos.

Selections from the Grand Opening, July 19, 1990:

Name: **LAZLO TOTH**
Address: **PO BOX 245**   Apt. _____

City: **FAIRFAX**   ZIP **94930**
State: **CALIFORNIA**

Gift card to be enclosed? **X** ____ If yes, please indicate name to be mentioned as the gift giver: **LAZLO TOTH** .

Item Code Quantity Description	Size/Color	Price	Total
			$ **10**
17) **Spaulding Golf Balls.** With the eagle logo in copper and green, and the President's signature. Sleeve of three: $10			**45**
51) **Birthplace Birdhouse.** A cozy re-creation of the Nixon boyhood home. Redesigned as Presidential quarters for your fine feathered friends. $45			____
52) **8 X 10 Photographs.** (All in color except RN and Elvis.) $5.50 per photo. (For additional photos see page 1.)			**5.50**
a. Presidents Bush and Nixon at the White House (1991).			**5.50**
g. The President and the King. (RN and Elvis at the White House, December 21, 1970.)			

Total Amount: $ **66.00**

Shipping and Handling: $ **14.57**

Tax (For Calif. orders only, add State Sales Tax of 7 3/4%): $ **5.11**

Gift box, ribbon, seal and card. ($2 per item boxed. Clearly indicate each item to be gift boxed.): $

Associates's Club Membership ($35 minimum): $ **35.01**

Total Due: $ **120.69**

$ 66.00
  7.75
——————
  330°00
  462°00
  462°00
——————
5.1 15000

18001 Yorba Linda Boulevard · Yorba Linda · California USA 92686
Telephone: (714) 993-3393 FAX: (714) 528-0544

Lazlo Toth
P.O. Box 245
Fairfax, California
94930 U.S.A.

October 14, 1991

Senator Joseph Biden Jr.
Chairman of the Judiciary Committee
United States Senate
Washington, D.C.

Dear Senator Chairman Biden,

Everybody says you were the best one on the Senate Sexual Harassment Committee Jury, and to this I agree. And even though you had an untimely root canal problem during the trial, you went on with your job just as though your teeth were normal. For this you deserve special commendation.

But I was shocked that you, the Chairman!, or any member of your committee, failed to apologize to the Coca-Cola company for dragging it's good name into the sordid testimony.

Professor Brenda Hill's statement, saying that Judge Clarence Thomas said, "Who has put pubic hair on my coke?", is one of the most disgusting, unappetizing things I have ever heard on National Television, and I doubt if they would even allow it to be said on a show like the Dating Game, but you let United State Senators repeat the phrase over and over again!

Why didn't you ask that the name "Coca-Cola", be stricken from the record and substituted for the general term, "Soft drink", so the official record would read, "Who has put pubic hair on my soft drink?"

Or why didn't any member of your committee ask, "Professor Hill, are you sure it was a Coke can? Could it have possibly been a Pepsi can? Or an R.C., or a Dr. Pepper? Are you sure it wasn't a Dr. Pepper and you were fantasizing it was a Coke?"

It seemed that all your committee cared about was talking about "pubic hairs" and "Long Dong Silver" and " big breasted women having sex with animals", while the good name of the greatest carbonated beverage to ever come out of the western world was taken in vain and dragged into the muck of the judiciary confirmation process! I know no one meant for this to happen, but happen it did, and an apology seems in order.

Best regards and here's hoping your dental problems are behind you.

Send me your picture,

Lazlo Toth

Lazlo Toth

Lazlo Toth
P.O. Box 245
Fairfax, California
94930 U.S.A.

October 14, 1991

Chairman of the Board
Coca-Cola Company
Atlanta, Georgia

To: The Chairman of the Board

Regarding: The "Pubic Hair on the Coke" reference during the senate
supreme court confirmation hearings:

We could spend hours discussing how Coca-Cola should handle this thing,
but frankly I think the best tactic to take is to completely ignore it.

All the best,

Lazlo Toth

The Coca-Cola Company

COCA-COLA PLAZA
ATLANTA, GEORGIA

EARL T. LEONARD, JR.
SENIOR VICE PRESIDENT

October 28, 1991

ADDRESS REPLY TO
P. O. DRAWER 1734
ATLANTA, GA. 30301
404 676-2622

Mr. Lazio Toth
P. O. Box 245
Fairfax, CA 94930

Dear Mr. Toth:

In response to your letter to Roberto Goizueta, the approach you suggest related to references to Coca-Cola in the recent confirmation hearings is the approach that we have taken. It was the obvious way to go.

Thanks for your interest in Coca-Cola, and for taking the time to write.

Sincerely,

ETLjr/mb

Unwavering Friendship Enterprises
Operation Desert Zoo

Lazlo Toth
Chief Coordinator

P.O. Box 245
Fairfax, California USA 94930

October 27, 1991

Defense Secretary Dick Cheyney
Department of Defense
Washington, D.C.

Dear Mr. Secretary,

Thank you for approving a medal for the civilians who supported and served in Operation Desert Storm. Also, thanks for keeping the cost down. $4.50 seems quite reasonable. From the picture of the medal in the paper, I would have guessed the cost would be more like five seventy-five.

New Civilian Medal For Gulf War Service

Associated Press

Washington
Defense Secretary Dick Cheney has approved a medal for the 4,000 civilians who served in the Persian Gulf during Operation Desert Shield and Operation Desert Storm, the Pentagon announced yesterday.

The medal is intended to "salute those civilians who made substantial contributions to the success of the operation while enduring many of the same hazards and conditions faced by military personnel," a Pentagon statement said.

All civilian Department of Defense employees who served in the Persian Gulf area of operations during the war are eligible to receive the medal. Also eligible are certain non-Defense Department workers who supported the war effort, such as the Red Cross, USO and Civil Reserve Air Fleet personnel, the statement said.

The medal design depicts a shield, a torch and crossed swords with the inscription "Desert Shield/Desert Storm."

"The shield is symbolic of a strong defense and military preparedness, while the torch, adapted from the Statue of Liberty, suggests leadership, freedom and relief from oppres-

BY UNITED PRESS INTERNATIONAL

The Pentagon will award this medal to 4,000 civilians

sion," the statement said. "The crossed swords represent cooperation and strength."

The Pentagon put the cost to produce the medal at $4.50 each. It is expected to be given to 4,000 civilians who served in the gulf war effort.

Secretary Cheyney, my participation in the Liberation of Kuwait was essentially in the civilian livestock arena. I was surprised to have my efforts to rebuild and restock the devastated Kuwait City Zoo acknowledged by the World Society for the Protecton of Animals, as well as The Sociedad Mundial para la Proteccion de los Animales, The Societe Mondiale pour la Protection des Animaux, and Weittierschutz-Gesellschaft. But never in a million years did I think I would be offered a medal. Thank-you!

Enclosed please find $4.50 cash.

Stand by our flag!

Lazlo Toth

Lazlo Toth

THE OFFICE OF THE ASSISTANT SECRETARY OF DEFENSE

WASHINGTON, D.C. 20301-4000

5 NOV 1991

**FORCE MANAGEMENT
AND PERSONNEL**

Mr. Lazlo Toth
Chief Coordinator,
Unwavering Friendship Enterprises
Operation Desert Zoo
P.O. Box 245
Fairfax, California 94930

Dear Mr. Toth;

Thank you very much for your kind letter of October 27, 1991, to Defense Secretary Cheney regarding the civilian Desert Shield/Desert Storm medal.

Regretfully, it appears that you have misinterpreted the newspaper article concerning the medal. The only non-Department of Defense employees eligible for the medal are Red Cross, USO, and Civilian Reserve Air Fleet personnel.

I regret that I am unable to provide a more favorable response to your inquiry. Your $4.50 is returned.

Sincerely,

PAUL T. ROSSBACH
Department of Defense Incentive Awards Administrator
Office of the Deputy Assistant Secretary of Defense
(Civilian Personnel Policy/Equal Opportunity)

OFFICE OF THE SECRETARY OF DEFENSE

MEMO FOR _____

Lazlo Toth
P.O. Box 245
Fairfax, California
94930 U.S.A.

October 29, 1991

Ticket Chairman
Dedication Committee
Ronald Reagan Presidential Library
Semi Valley, California

Dear Sir:

I just read in the paper that President Reagan's Library is being dedicated on November 4th, and I hope it's not too late to get a ticket.

There will only be one in my party (myself), so there's no need to send two tickets since I'm traveling alone. I tried to talk some friends of mine in my prayer group into coming along but everyone says it's too far, so I'll be driving alone, that's why I only need one ticket.

Also, I need directions. I know I take 101 South, but then what? Where do I turn, that's what I need to know.

Also, I would like to know if food will be served, or, if not, if you have a cafeteria or dining facilities. If the answer to both questions is "no', I'll bring my own food. Which leads me to question number three: Do you at least have picnic tables? The big flaw of President Nixon's library, besides leaving out the Pope in his Hall of Life Size World Leaders, is that there are no eating facilities. You look at all the beautiful statues of world leaders and get to listen to all the wonderful tapes, and then, if you're hungry, you have to go to Denny's if you want something to eat. It doesn't make sense!

Looking forward to the 4th!

Lazlo Toth

Lazlo Toth

P.S.
I am happy to report that I have a historic picture of President Reagan from years ago that I would like to donate to the library, but instead of taking a chance and mailing it, I'll bring it with me and donate it in person.

95008-44

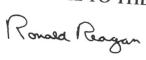

Dedication
1991

40 Presidential Drive
Simi Valley, California 93065

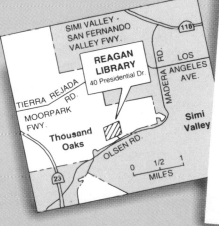

SIMI VALLEY -
SAN FERNANDO
VALLEY FWY.

118

**REAGAN
LIBRARY**
40 Presidential Dr.

LOS
ANGELES
AVE.

MADERA RD.

TIERRA REJADA RD.

MOORPARK
FWY.

**Thousand
Oaks**

OLSEN RD.

**Simi
Valley**

23

0   1/2   1
MILES

GEORGE BUSH
WASHINGTON, D.C.

October 23, 1991

Lazlo Toth
Box 245
Fairfax, CA 94978-0245

Dear Friend,

I wanted you personally to know that I have just authorized the formation of the "Bush - Quayle '92" Committee.

In the next few months, I will officially announce my decision whether or not to seek the Presidency for a second term.

But before I make that final announcement, I wanted to ask you a very important question:

Lazlo, can I count on you to become one of the first members of the "Bush - Quayle '92" campaign from California?

I know, from your past record of support, that you share many of the same values, dreams and goals that Vice-President Dan Quayle and I have been working so hard to achieve.

Indeed, it is because you have shown yourself to be such a loyal friend that it is very important to me to know that I will be able to turn to you again for help.

But first I want to ask you the very special favor of please letting me know as quickly as possible whether you will be accepting my invitation.

By accepting this invitation you will participate in what I personally believe will be one of the most historic, most important elections our Nation has faced in the past 75 years.

You see, the 1992 election will be much more than simply a race for the White House. It will also be a campaign to elect a Congress that is, at last, in step with the wishes, dreams and hopes of the American people.

In short, I see the 1992 election as a national referendum for choosing the leaders -- and setting the direction -- of our Nation for the balanc   is century.

Here   will decide whether or not we finally
make a cl   ess' bankrupt high tax and
big-spend   dom

And   loving p
reaffirm

But if we are to wage the kind of campaign that will energize America, bring voters to the polls, and win not just the White House but a sweeping Republican victory in Congress as well, we are all going to have to work harder and do more than ever before.

So if you can generously support our efforts, I want to urge you with all my heart to please do so. I will personally pledge to you that, in addition to running the strongest campaign I am capable of, I will also do everything I can to help our GOP candidates all over this Nation come home to victory in 1992.

You've helped me and our Party in the past. I am hoping you will stand with me again.

In the next few months I will officially announce my decision to seek the Presidency for a second term. But before I make the final announcement, I wanted to write to you and ask you for your help.

I am looking forward to hearing from you as soon as possible.

Sincerely,

George Bush

P.S. I can't stress enough how important your quick response is to my letter. At this point, overcoming complacency and over-confidence is our biggest hurdle. Please write back to me today. Thank you.

BUSH 92 QUAYLE
★ ★ ★ ★ ★ ★ ★ ★ ★ ★ ★ ★

A Reply To The President

Dear Mr. President,

I am deeply honored by and I accept your invitation to become one of the first official members of your re-election campaign in my state.

To make sure America continues on the steady course you have set us on, I am making my membership contribution in the amount indicated below.

The Membership Levels

The Bush - Quayle '92 campaign has established six membership levels: Gold, Silver and Bronze... and Red, White and Blue. You'll receive a prestigious lapel pin bearing the color of your membership level. More than becoming a prized collector's item, which these pins will most assuredly become, they will afford you the special recognition you deserve as one of our first campaign members.

/ /$1,000 - Gold / /$500 - Silver / /$100 - Bronze
/ /$75 - Red / /$50 - White / /$35 - Blue / /$_____Other

Please make check payable to Bush - Quayle '92 Primary Committee, Inc.

K400 802750

```
Lazlo Toth
Box 245
Fairfax, CA  94978 0245
```

Dear President Bush,

I was deeply moved by your letter asking me to join your re-election team. Yes!, you can count on me to become one of the first members of the "Bush-Quale '92" campaign.

One question: Mr. President, does the GOLD $1000 lapel pin contain any real gold? I'm allergic to gold and am hoping by "Gold" you mean the color gold, and not the metal.

I am looking forward to hearing from you as soon as possible,

Lazlo Toth

Lazlo Toth

Lazlo Toth
P.O. Box 245
Fairfax, California
94930 U.S.A.

November 3, 1991

President
V-8 Juice Company
Camden, N.J.
08103-1701

Dear President of V-8 Juice,

On Halloween, instead of giving out candy, I offered Trick or Treaters a choice of small cans of juice - V-8, Tomatoe, or Pineapple. And I would like to report to you that 60% asked for V-8!

Congradulations!

Lazlo Toth

Lazlo Toth

Campbell Soup Company

December 15, 1991

Mr. Lazlo Toth
P. O. Box 245
Fairfax, CA 94930

Dear Mr. Toth,

    Thank you for taking the time to give us such kind and thoughtful comments. We appreciate hearing both positive and negative comments from our consumers, and yours were particularly rewarding.

    For over 100 years, we at Campbell's have worked to make the best products available at an economical price. Compliments like yours help us feel that we are achieving that goal.

    Since you are interested in good food, I am enclosing a coupon for one of our Campbell products and some of our favorite recipe suggestions. I hope you enjoy them.

Sincerely,
Florence Boskey
Consumer Correspondent

NO REPLY !

P. O. Box 245
Fairfax, California
94930
November 6, 1991

President
United Airlines
P.O. Box 66100
Chicago, Illinois 60666

Dear Sir,

   After I wrote to you on September 15, I received a letter back from your Customer Relations Department and I think they misunderstood my question.   When I wrote to you and asked, "Why is the food so bad?", I was not referring to any one particular meal on any one particular flight. I was commenting on your food in general.

   If the meals "meet your customers' expectations", like your Customer Relations Department claims, it's only because their expectations of an airplane meal are so low to begin with.
   If you asked someone who was stuck in a well if the food that was lowered down to them "met their expectations", they would probably say "Yes", too.   Do I make my point?

    I happen to be in the food industry myself, and I know it's not easy to prepare precooked dinners, especially for high altitude dining.
And I'm sure it's not cheap. I would guess that an average inflight dinner like the Lasagne, or Beef Stroganoff, cost you at least $5.95. Plus you have the washing the silverware costs, which probably adds another thirty-five cents per unit. Total cost per meal: $6.30!
   That's why I would like to suggest at this time my idea for a Two Pronged Ticket Price System. Regular price (and 500 Bonus miles) for those who choose to eat the food prepared by your Food Service Department - The "United Frequent Eater Fare", and a new "United BYOF Fare" - a lower fare for people who wish to purchase their in flight meals elsewhere and carry their own food and utensils on board.

        Your bathrooms are small, but they're well lit,

        Lazlo Toth
        Lazlo Toth

The Honorable James Baker
Secretary of State
The State Department
Washington, D.C.

11-11-91

Lazlo Toth
P.O. Box 245
Fairfax, California
94930 U.S.A.

Dear Secretary Baker,

   Congradulations! Even though the first meeting of the Middle East peace talks in Madrid didn't end up with all the delegates shaking hands and trading home phone numbers, it was a significant first step, and for this you deserve great credit.
   Being a peacemaker is a difficult and lonely task. How well I know! Although I am not a licensed, accredited diplomat, I, too, have been working on a Plan for Peace in the Middle East. Although my plan is simple, it involves significant financing, and because I am an individual, private citizen, the McArthur Foundation is unable, at this time, under present tax laws, to fund my plan. Catch 22!

   Mr. Secretary, since you already cracked the ice in Madrid, I am willing at this time to sacrifice individual glory (and a possible medal) and turn my plan over to the American government. Since King Hussein of Jordan backed Saddam in Operation Desert Storm, and since thousands of Palestinians already live in Jordan, why not invite all Palestinians to move there?
   My plan is to make Jordan the new Palestinian homeland, and relocate the King, his American wife and staff to the most royal residence in the United States - Elvis Presley's GRACELAND, in Memphis, Tennessee!

   I have been unable to nail down a firm asking price for Graceland, but besides the cost of the property, we should be prepared to pay to relocate the Presley enterprises (including gift shop, cars and costumes) to Elvis' birthplace in Tupelo, (estimate cost - $1 million), plus compensate the Presley family for disturbing their way of life and tour schedules ($5 million?). Also, we should be prepared to reimburse the Husseins for air fare and transportation to and from airports.

   Perhaps we can get President Nixon, a personal friend of both Elvis and the King, to break the news to the Husseins about being transfered to Memphis. Another option is to move them to Panama where we sent the Shah, but "A King deserves a King's home", that's what he can tell him.

          Full speed ahead,

          Lazlo Toth   Lazlo Toth

Mario Lanza Fan Club

A Non-Denominational, Non-Partisan organization devoted to keeping the memory and recordings of Mario Lanza alive in the Western World and Canada.

Box 245 / Fairfax, California / 94930

November 22, 1991

Vice President Dan Quale
The White House
Washington, D.C.

Dear Mr. Vice President:

    I have recently become one of the first official members of the BUSH '92 re-election campaign in California.

    In 1988 I campaigned on your behalf in my district.

    Other members of the Mario Lanza Fan Club also supported your candidacy.

    Mr. Vice President, we are more than quite upset that you made fun of the name "Mario" during your recent T.V. (television) appearances.
Mr. Vice President, that was uncalled for!

    We know Mario Cuomo was the "Mario" you were referring to, but you slurred the name "Mario" not "Cuomo"! MARIO!, the first name of the greatest opera singer to ever live!

    Furthermore, the name Mario is the male equivalent of MARIA, the name of the Mother of Jesus, and a lot of Christians don't like you making fun of the name of the male equivalent of the Mother of God! I also would like to point out to you that the name "MARILYN", your own wife's name, is a derivative of MARIA, the female equivalent of MARIO, the name you're making fun of!

    Mr. Vice President, you're in enough trouble with the Doonesberry accusations and with the House Operations Committee investigating your staff. You don't need this!

M. L. Toth

M. Lazlo Toth
Vice-President

■ **MAR-I-O** — Vice President Dan Quayle thinks New York Governor Mario Cuomo will be the final presidential choice among Democrats come July.
"It's going to be friend Mar-i-o," he told reporters at a breakfast yesterday, stretching out the vowels.

BUSH 92 QUAYLE
★ ★ ★ ★ ★ ★ ★ ★ ★ ★ ★

BOBBY HOLT
National Finance Chairman

December 2, 1991

Lazlo Toth
Box 245
Fairfax, CA 94978-0245

Dear Friend,

In recognition of the loyal and steadfast support you have given President Bush, it is an honor for me to present you with the enclosed Bush-Quayle '92 Certificate of Appreciation.

Your extraordinary commitment to the democratic principles and traditional values that are so important to the President and all of us has earned you the respect and admiration of everyone involved in planning President Bush's last campaign.

That is why we're counting heavily on your support as President Bush and Vice President Quayle prepare for what will soon become a grueling battle against the Democrats in 1992.

I hope you will frame and display with great pride this award which you so richly deserve. Though I must tell you, it is but a token of the President's appreciation for your loyalty and faith through the years.

Just knowing you are behind the President has been an incredible source of strength for him during the difficult times our na. And knowing you share our joy when we achievistory that much more meanin

E
emotic

role
leade
with

-- a
Fath
hist

Certificate of Appreciation

PRESENTED THIS DAY TO

Lazlo Toth

IN RECOGNITION OF EXTRAORDINARY SERVICE AND UNEQUALED PERSONAL COMMITMENT TO THE PRESIDENT AND VICE PRESIDENT OF THE UNITED STATES IN THEIR 1992 NATIONAL CAMPAIGN FOR RE-ELECTION.

SIGNED, WITNESSED AND PRESENTED THIS 2ND DAY OF DECEMBER, NINETEEN HUNDRED AND NINETY-ONE BY

BOBBY HOLT
National Finance Chairman

BUSH 92 QUAYLE
★ ★ ★ ★ ★ ★ ★

J. STANLEY HUCKABY
Treasurer

Lazlo Toth
P.O. Box 245
Fairfax, California
94930 U.S.A.

December 5, 1991

John Sununu
Advisor to the President
The White House
Washington, D.C.

Dear Mr. Sununu,

When the going gets tough, the tough get going - and the weak fire their subordinates.

Everybody knows that if President Bush's popularity ratings were going up instead of down you would still be Chief of Staff!

In today's world, the Captain may still go down with the ship, but the co-captain is always offered to the sea first.

At least you've still got your stamp collection and I'm sure you'll be offered a great book deal like Ollie North. I bought his, and I'll buy yours, - that's for sure!

Lazlo Toth

Lazlo Toth

UNDER FIRE

THE WHITE HOUSE

WASHINGTON

December 23, 1991

Dear Mr. Toth,

Thank you for your kind message and words of support
and encouragement. I feel honored to have been part of
these past three years of the President's first term in
office and look forward to new challenges in the
future.

I appreciate very much your taking the time to write.

Sincerely,

John H. Sununu
Counsellor to the President

Mr. Lazlo Toth
Post Office Box 245
Fairfax, California 94930

12-17-91   Christmas 1991

Dear Mr & Mrs Bush —

Wishing you
a year that's filled
With lots of happy things. re-election
Beginning with
the special joy
That Christmas always brings!

Merry Christmas
and a Happy New Year
1992 they will call it!

Laszlo Toth

P.S.
Last year at this time you had
Saddam breathing down your neck —
this year all you've got is Cuomo!
(you can use that)

The Family Tree.
Upstairs at the White House

The President and Mrs. Bush
extend their warmest wishes
that you and your loved ones
will share a joyous Christmas
and a peaceful new year.

1991

Lazlo Toth
P.O. Box 245
Fairfax, California
94930 U.S.A.

December 28, 1991

GALLUP POLL/*MOST ADMIRED*

Hon. Margaret Thrasher
Former Prime Minister of England
House of Lords
London, England (GREAT BRITAIN)

My Dear Former Prime MInister

    Congradulations! Enclosed is the latest Gallup Poll and you are #3, right behind the First Lady of the Land, Barbara Bush (#1), and the Albanian (Former KGB Mole), Mother Teresa (#2). You were way ahead of your rival, Onaphera Winfrey (#6), and left Queen Elizabeth Windsor in the dust (#8).

Now that you are out of office
I hope that you can find the time
to send me your picture.

All the best of regards
and Happy New Year
New Years Wishes
to all the Lords and Commoners.

Your Cousin,

Laslo Toth

Lazlo Toth

MOST ADMIRED WOMEN
1. Barbara Bush
2. Mother Teresa
3. Margaret Thatcher
4. Nancy Reagan
5. Oprah Winfrey
6. Jackie Kennedy Onassis
7. Elizabeth Taylor
8. Queen Elizabeth
9. Sandra Day O'Connor
10. Betty Ford

THE RT. HON. MARGARET THATCHER, O.M., F.R.S., M.P.

10th February 1992

Dear Mr Troth,

I am writing on behalf of Mrs Thatcher to thank you for your recent letter.

As requested I enclose a photograph of Mrs Thatcher which I hope you will like.

With best wishes,

Yours sincerely,

M. Cracroft

MISS MIRANDA CRACROFT
Private Office

Mr L Toth

Lazlo Toth
P.O. Box 245
Fairfax, California
94930 U.S.A.

December 27, 1991

Rep. Louis Stokes (Dem-Ohio)
Chairman of the House Select Committee on Presidential Assassinations
House of Representatives
Washington, D.C.

Dear Congressman Stokes,

I read in the paper that you said there is no reason to open the remaining sealed files pertaining to the assassination of President Kennedy.
For this, I thank you. Why does everybody have to know everything about everything in their own lifetime? What's the big deal?
President Bush said when he was Director of the CIA he didn't even LOOK at the Kennedy Assassination File because he was so convinced that The Warren Comminssion Report was correct in it's findings.

Personally, I agree with both of you that Oswald was the lone gunman, but I always adhered to the theory that Governor Connally was his true target, and that he was just a bad shot. But lately, I heard a rumor that the Super 8 camera Abraham Zapruder used to film the assassination actually belonged to Lee Harvey Oswald (they were roommates in the Marine Corp), and that Oswald was so angry that Zapruder took his camera without asking his permission, that he grabbed a rifle and went to the top of the book despository building to look for him in the crowd. He fired at Zapruder just when the Connally-Kennedy limo was going by.
Now, I'm not sure which of the stories to believe, but one thing I know for sure is that Oswald was the lone gun man and that he acted alone. Why can't people just believe that? Didn't these people read the Warren Commission Report?

Now, finally, the truth is out that President Harding actually choked to death on a pretzel, and the rumors that he was poisoned by his wife can be put to bed. What difference would it have made if people knew about the pretzel back in 1923? The truth will come out eventually, what's the rush? You and I and President Bush all agree on this.

Keep the files closed!

Lazlo Toth

Lazlo Toth

LOUIS STOKES
21ST DISTRICT, OHIO

CHAIRMAN,
COMMITTEE ON STANDARDS
OF OFFICIAL CONDUCT

MEMBER,
COMMITTEE ON APPROPRIATIONS

SUBCOMMITTEES:
LABOR/HHS/EDUCATION
HUD/INDEPENDENT AGENCIES
DISTRICT OF COLUMBIA

Congress of the United States
House of Representatives
Washington, DC 20515-3521

2365 RAYBURN HOUSE OFFICE BUILDING
WASHINGTON, DC 20515-3521
(202) 225-7032

DISTRICT OFFICE:
ROOM 2947
NEW FEDERAL OFFICE BUILDING
1240 EAST 9TH STREET
CLEVELAND, OH 44199
(216) 522-4900

CLEVELAND HEIGHTS OFFICE
2140 LEE ROAD
SUITE 211
CLEVELAND HEIGHTS, OH 44118
(216) 522-4907

January 29, 1992

Mr. Lazio Toth
P.O. Box 245
Fairfax, California 94930

Dear Mr. Toth:

Thank you for your letter urging the release of the sealed
files in the John F. Kennedy investigation by the House
Select Committee on Assassinations, of which I served as
Chairman.

This is to advise you that, when the Committee which I
chaired completed its work in the investigation of the
assassination of President John F. Kennedy, we released 12
volumes of information regarding our investigation, which
were available to the American public. Additionally we
held in excess of fifteen days of nationally publicized and
televised hearings of the results of our investigation.
With regard to the assassination of President Kennedy, our
committee began its work thirteen years after the death of
the President.

The records pertaining to our committee's investigation
were sealed by the House of Representatives, in accordance
with a rule of the House of Representatives concerning
unpublished House Committee Records. These records were
not sealed pursuant to any effort to conceal any of the
facts and circumstances pertaining to the assassination of
President John F. Kennedy.

I deem it unfortunate that people are being led to believe
that the records sealed by the House of Representatives
pertaining to our investigation have covered up facts
pertaining to the assassination of the President. I also
deem it a disservice to our committee to have its good work
impugned by persons who have never read or studied our
publicly released reports and who are led to believe that
any information not contained in our reports in some way
covers up government involvement in the assassination of
the President. Indeed, it is unfortunate that most people
have not taken the time to read the results of our
investigation which were printed by the United States
Government Printing Office and made available to the
public.

Consequently I am now in the process of initiating action
in the House and Senate, to release not only the records
of the committee which I chaired but also records of other
committees and agencies which have sealed records
pertaining to the assassination of the President. I am
proceeding as expeditiously as possible with the hope that
the release of such records can be accomplished in the
current Congress.

I appreciate your taking the time to express your interest
in this matter.

Sincerely,

LOUIS STOKES
Member of Congress

Box 245 Fairfax, California 94930

December 30, 1991

President
Safeway Grocery Stores
Safeway Grocery Stores Headquarters
47400 Kato Rd.
Freemont, California

Dear Sir:

I am a customer of your store located in the Red Hill Shopping Center down the road from the Miracle Mile, in San Anselmo, California. Although I live in Fairfax, almost two miles away, I buy groceries at Safeway because it's in the same shopping as a Pet Store that buys my home made flea powder. I know you're probably thinking that I want to sell my flea powder to Safeway, that's why I'm writing, but that is not the case. I only mention the flea powder because it's the reason I shop way over there instead of at a store closer to my home.

I would like to report that your Red Hill store is excellent with one major exception. In the dairy case, they always put the freshest milk way in the back, behind the older milk, where it's hard to reach. I've complained, but they keep doing it!

The last time I was there (yesterday), I knocked over some of the cartons up front, (which were stamped "Jan 05"), when I was reaching for one in the back (stamped "Jan 09"), and one of your employees made it seem like I had committed the mortal sin of the century just because I wanted the most currently dated carton of milk and didn't fall for his little trick of taking the one up front.

I know, "it's ALL fresh", and maybe a couple of days of freshness difference doesn't matter to some people (him), but it does to others (me), and your employees shouldn't make your customers have to reach and strain and perhaps knock over other cartons, just because we want to buy the freshest milk available.

You let customer choose what kind of bag they want - "Plastic or Paper", let us choose the milk we want without getting hernias in the process!

Paper!

Lazlo Toth
Lazlo Toth

**SAFEWAY** INC.
47400 KATO ROAD
FREMONT, CA 94538

January 13, 1992

Mr. Lazlo Toth
P.O. Box 245
Fairfax, CA 94930

Dear Mr. Toth:

Thank you for your letter regarding the placement of milk in
the dairy case at our San Anselmo store.

It is common practice in the industry to place the most
current dated product in the front of the case so as to
encourage its purchase. However, we understand your concern,
which will be reviewed by our operations managers.

Mr. Toth, thank you for taking the time to write. We value
your patronage and trust we will continue to serve you.

Sincerely,

Debra Lambert
Public Relations Manager
Northern California Division

DML:jff

cc: Mike Daniels, District Manager

Recycled
Paper

January 11, 1992

Mr. Harold Poling
President
Ford Motor Company
Detroit, Michigan

Lazlo Toth
P.O. Box 245
Fairfax, California
94930 U.S.A.

Dear Red,

Welcome back from Japan, and a million thanks for traveling all that way with President Bush and the CEO's of GM and Chrysler to help iron out our trade problems.

I know you're a little disappointed with the outcome, but I think you did a wonderful job bargaining with the Japanese! You shouldn't be so hard on yourself!

As I read the deal, the Japanese have agreed to lower their safety standards so 20,000 more American cars per year can get in, and because they drive on the wrong side of the road, they want the cars we export to them to have the steering wheel on the right side of the car.

I know you hate to give in to them on the steering wheel issues, but I think there's a spin we could put on it so we don't lose face. Why not announce that starting in '93, all American automobiles exported to Japan will feature the glove compartment on the left side of the car, and because of this innovative glove compartment design change, the placement of the steering wheel will be adjusted slightly to the right.

Wipe those tears off the dashboard!
Fight! Fight! Fight!

Lazlo

Lazlo Toth

Susan F. Shackson
Director
Public Policy Office

Ford Motor Company
The American Road
P.O. Box 1899
Dearborn, Michigan 48121

February 3, 1992

Mr. Lazlo Toth
P.O. Box 245
Fairfax, California 94930

Dear Mr. Toth:

Thank you for your letter. I appreciate your taking the time to
share your thoughts and concerns with us.

We were disappointed in what we view as some inaccurate
interpretations by the media of the auto industry's objectives in
accompanying the President to Japan. Our goal, and that of the
Administration, was to demonstrate that U.S. government and
business are cooperating and are extremely concerned about the
imbalance in our trading relationship.

Thank you again for taking the time to share your thoughts with us.

Sincerely,

Susan F. Shackson

January 11, 1992

Mr. Lee Iacocca
Chairman
Chrysler Corporation
Detroit, Michigan

Lazlo Toth
P.O. Box 245
Fairfax, California
94930 U.S.A.

Dear Mr. Iacocca,

I am one American who is sick and tired of all the Big Three Bashing that went on in the press while you and the other car company executives were in Japan! All they wrote about was how much money you make and how you guys make five times as much as your Japanese counterparts. And they make a big deal of the fact that a Japanese CEO will cut his pay before he lays off any workers. (They don't mention the fact that the same guy will probably commit Hari-Kari if somebody were to find out he was late for a Dental appointment.)

I agree with you 100% that "we don't have idiots running General Motors, Ford and Chrysler". If you're all idiots, how come you make so much more money than the men who are running car companies that are making money? Let them answer that one! Come on!

Mr. Chairman, I have an idea for you that you might want to run up the flagpole at the next Board of Directors Meeting:

How about giving a $1000 cash rebate and an American flag to anyone who trades in their Japanese car for a new Chrysler or Dodge!

THEN, (step #2) - How about selling all the used trade-ins back to the Japanese! Since they love their own cars so much, why not use Japanese trade-ins to solve the Japanese trade problem? Why should Chrysler fight the uphill battle of selling American cars to the Japanese, when you can sell them Japanese cars instead?

This plan, this spirit!, will not only put more American cars back on American roads, but it will take Japanese cars off of them! It will not only put more American flags on American flag poles, but it will drastically reduce the $41 Billion Japanese trade deficit. It will not only put $1000 cash in new Chrysler owners pockets, but it could act as a launching pad for your bid for the Presidency, should you decide to take a drastic $4.2 Million pay cut and run.

Japanese cars go home!
I Like Iac!

Lazlo Toth

Chrysler Corporation
Chrysler Center

February 3, 1992

Mr. Lazlo Toth
P.O. Box 245
Fairfax, CA 94930

Dear Mr. Toth:

Thank you for your letter to Mr. Lee A. Iacocca. He appreciates the time and effort you put into it and would like to respond to you personally. Unfortunately, the large number of letters he receives every day makes it impossible for him to answer as many as he would like. Therefore, he has asked me to reply.

We are sensitive to the needs and expectations of consumers and are continuously looking for ways to meet them. We did a preliminary evaluation of your suggestions to determine if they might meet these needs and expectations. Based on our findings, we regret that we are unable to incorporate your suggestions into our plans at this time.

Thank you again for writing. We appreciate your suggestion and your interest in Chrysler.

Sincerely,

M. D. Kane
Special Projects Manager
Marketing Group

January 11, 1992

Lazlo Toth
P.O. Box 245
Fairfax, California
94930 U.S.A.

Robert Stempel, CEO
 General Motors
"The Big One"
Detroit, Michigan

Dear CEO Stempel,

Welcome back from Japan and thanks for speaking up for America instead of always whining like the leaches in the press corp. Instead of supporting the AMerican auto industry, they prefer to pick on you, pointing out things like the fact that even though General Motors is losing money, you still get a salary of over $2 million a year ($2,189,000). I for one think you deserve every dollar of your salary, and I'm glad for you that you're not working on commission! Do you get that one?

Sir!, speaking of working on commission, I have a point to make.
It concerns the manner in which you sell your cars.
I believe if you paid your salesmen weekly salaries instead of making them scrape and claw for commissions, it would be a lot more pleasant experience to shop for a car. Now, going to one of your "showrooms" is like having to go into the shark tank! The salesmen are all buddy-buddy when they're just smoking and hanging around alone together, but when a customer walks in, they act like starving turkey buzzards flying towards the only decaying squirrell in the forrest. Sometimes they don't even let you get into the door
  they attack you in the parking lot! And then they try to take you to one of their little rooms where they want to bargain with you like you were buying a camel instead of a new american automobile - the proudest machine to ever be invented! Sir, your salesmen may be sharks, but they are sharks dogpaddling for their lives! Why not give them a weekly wage like most of the other GM people (including you) receive? Maybe if you had a "set" price on your cars (like TV sets), and your desperate sales staff didn't attack people in the parking lot, you would sell more cars!

I've deceided to keep my car for another year,

Lazlo Toth
Lazlo Toth

General Motors Corporation
March 17, 1992

ROBERT H. OGDEN
GENERAL DIRECTOR
Sales Operations and
Dealer Relations

Mr. Lazio Toth
P.O. Box 245
Fairfax, CA 94930

Dear Mr. Toth:

Bob Stempel, General Motors Chairman, has forwarded your recent letter to me and asked that I respond for him.

We want to thank you for your kind comments and your support of our efforts in the American auto industry.

With regard to your suggestions on paying retail salespeople salaries rather than commissions, General Motors has no control over this. The salespeople are employed by the dealers, who are independent businesspeople. I am aware of some dealerships that do pay their salespeople a salary rather than commissions, but I think the vast majority are on a commission plan.

Also, all too often we receive letters with comments such as yours about unpleasant experiences in the showroom. They range from customers being ignored to being treated rudely.

We presently have several programs in progress to raise the professionalism of our retail salespeople. They include training, skills and product knowledge certification testing, and career enhancement programs, all designed to help GM dealers attract and retain the best salespeople in the industry. Also, many of our dealerships are presently trying a fixed price sales approach which eliminates the haggling that so many buyers dislike.

One thing that is certain in this competitive marketplace we are currently in -- dealers as well as manufacturers that do not treat customers right, both in sales and service, will not survive.

Thank you again for taking the time to write and for your comments and input. They are very much appreciated.

Sincerely,

Bob Ogden

General Motors Building 3044 West Grand Boulevard Detroit, Michigan 48202

P. O. Box 245
Fairfax, California
9 4 9 3 0
January 12, 1991

President
Preparation H
Whitehall Laboratories
New York, New York

Dear Mr. President,

    I have seen commercials for your product on television and I have but one question - What does the "H" stand for?

Laslo Toth

Lazlo Toth

WHITEHALL LABORATORIES

Division of American Home Products Corporation

685 THIRD AVENUE, NEW YORK, NEW YORK 10017-4076

EXECUTIVE OFFICES   (212) 878-5500

January 30, 1992

Mr. Lazio Toth
P.O. Box 245
Fairfax, CA 94930

Dear Mr. Toth:

Thank you for your recent letter concerning Preparation H.

Please be advised that H stands for hemorrhoids.

Sincerely,

Cecelia McDonnell
Manager, Consumer Affairs

CMC/af

Singapore Cracks Down on Gum

No importing, no selling, no chewing — especially in the subway

President   January 17, 1992
Wrigley's Chewing Gum Company
The Wrigley's Building   **Box 245 Fairfax, California 94930**
Chicago, Illinois

Dear Sir,

Years ago I visited Chicago and was most impressed by your beautiful skyscraper building. As far as I know, no other Gum or Candy Bar has it's own building. There is no Bazooka Building! There is no Reese's Cup Building! Only Wrigley's Gum has it's own building - The Wrigley's Building!

And the same goes for baseball fields! Once someone told me the reason the Chicago ball park is named Wrigley's Field is because of all the gum underneath the seats. But later I found out the Gum Company owned the ball park, too! No other gum, as far as I know, owns a ball park either. There is no Dentyne Field! There is no Trident Field! Only, Wrigley's Field!

It's a good thing your ball park isn't located in Sinagapore! I'm enclosing a headline from an article in the newspaper about how they're banning chewing gum because "spent" gum is causing their subway doors from closing. You'd think the spent gum climbed up on those subway doors all by itself! I say don't blame the chewing gum, blame the gum chewer! Those people probably even put gum underneath the chairs in their own homes! Anyway, you can stop worrying about losing the lucrative Singapore market because I have good tidings!

Three and a half years ago, I was presented a formula that makes gum unstickable. This formula, which I credit to the intercession of Fr. Junipero Serra, is currently possibly being researched by a Vatican canonical investigative team. Meanwhile, I wish to offer this knowledge to you.

My <u>MIRACLE FORMULA 280</u> is not an ingredient or an additive, but a simple, five minute process that makes chewing gum lose its elastic quality, and incapacitates it's ability to stick to ANYTHING!

My Three Step (one stick) Program involves:
1. chewing the gum forty (40) times on the right side of the mouth. Then -
2. chewing the gum forty (40) times on the left side of the mouth. Then -
3. chewing the gum on both sides of the mouth, back and forth, for two
    hundred (200) times, starting on the left side.

I know this 280 Chew Process may require a little effort, and take some of the glamour out of chewing Chewing Gum, but after you have tested the Formula you will find that it works, that's all I can say.   Lazlo Toth

Lazlo Toth

Unwavering Friendship Enterprises
Operation Desert Zoo

Lazlo Toth
Chief Coordinator

P.O. Box 245
Fairfax, California USA 94930

January 20, 1992

Saud Nasir al-Sabah
Kuwaiti Ambassador to the United States
Kuwait Embassy / 2940 Tilden Street NW
Washington, D.C.

Dear Mr. Ambassador,

On the first anniversary of Operation Desert Storm we should be celebrating, instead <u>60 Minutes</u> reported last night that the moving story the young Kuwait girl told before the congressional panel about Iraqi soldiers pulling babies out of incubators, was "untrue".

Also, they made a big deal out of the fact that she turned out to be a member of the Kuwait Royal Family (and your daughter), and that nobody on the committee mentioned that at the time of the hearings.

Frankly, I think she did a wonderful job! - and evidently a lot of congressmen did too! Her dramatic story was one of the main reasons why congress voted to go to war. As you know, the vote was very, very close, and without her story, Operation Desert Storm may never have happened! Saddam is still in charge in Iraq, but if it wasn't for that tearful story, you and the rest of the royal family would probably be living on some boat docked in the bay in Monte Carlo, and the population of Iraq probably would have gone up, instead of down by 200,000! So, Congradulations to you!, your daughter!, your Father-in-law (The Emir!), and especially the talented American! public relations firm you hired to help you get the American people, and their representatives, to believe the phony story.

Mr. Ambassador!, I am worried that next thing they'll be telling us on <u>60 Minutes</u> is that the Zoo Atrocities didn't really happen either! Please reassure me that my efforts to restock the Kuwait City Zoo were not in vain.

Unwaveringly yours,

Lazlo Toth

Lazlo Toth

NO REPLY !

Lazlo Toth
P.O. Box 245
Fairfax, California
94930 U.S.A.

January 23, 1992

Imelda Marcos
Marcos for President Headquarters
Manila,The Phillipines

Dear Imelda,

Please forgive the informality, but I feel I know you. And not just slightly - I feel I know you very, very well!

Again! last night, I dreamed that I was your Dentist.

And, once again, in my dream, we had more than a Dentist-patient relationship, if you know what I mean!

Once again, I didn't even charge you for the visit, not even for the X-rays I took, even though I have a lot of overhead.

Imelda! Imelda! Just typing your name, I begin to shake!

I have written many letters over the years, but I must admit, I have never been more nervous when writing to ANYONE, as I am now to you. I know why ofcourse. It's because of your beauty. No one else can send off the bells of romance, like you do to me, each time I am lucky enough to run across a new photograph of you in the newspaper.

Yesterday morning was no exception, although I must admit I felt a tinge of jealousy when I read that you said you found Saddam Hussein "a very attractive man". Everyone has read about your affairs with the Rat Pack and the singing group, ABBA, but it still was a shocker to read that you admitted visiting Saddam (or one of his Look-Alikes), "several times", while you were first Lady of the Phillipines.

Am I shocked? Frankly, yes! But, regardless!, my feelings only grow! "Something must be wrong with me! ", is what I told Shannon, the waitress at the Koffee Klatch. She said she knows exactly what I'm going through, and that she gets the same feelings everytime she sees a picture of a fellow named "Gallagher" in the newspaper.   At least it gives me some assurances that somethings not wrong just with me!

Imelda!, Emerald of the People!, Flower of the Phillipines!, I am sending along a small ($1) contribution, to help you on your road back to the royal palace. If I could, I would buy you the Buster Brown Company!

Send me your picture! I beg of you!

Lazlo

Lazlo Toth

P.O. Box 245
Fairfax, California
U.S.A. 94930
January 24, 1992

Consumer Consultant
Ms. Monti Trent-Zinn
Kellogg Company
Battle Creek, Michigan 49016

Dear Ms. Trent-Zinn,

I don't know if you remember me or not. Years ago I almost won the Rice-to-Riches contest. I know I haven't written to you much since then, but I need a favor from Kellogg's and you're the only person I know there.

I have an idea for a full length feature movie based on the lives of Snap!, Crackle! and Pop!, - and what I need to know from you at this time is - what is their last name?

Good morning!

Lazlo Toth

Lazlo Toth

Kellogg's

Mr. Lazlo Toth
PO Box 245
Fairfax, CA 94930

February 13, 1992

Dear Mr. Toth:

I am enclosing a fact sheet on Snap! Crackle! Pop! which I hope you will find useful. I am sorry to tell you that these characters were never given a last name.

Thank-you for contacting us.

Sincerely,

Linda J. Pell

Linda J. Pell
Manager
Consumer Affairs Department

Snap! Crackle! Pop!

Snap!® Crackle!® Pop!® appeared on the very first *Kellogg's® Rice Krispies®* cereal. In Sweden, they say "Piff! Paff! Puff!"; in Germany, "Knisper! Knasper! Knusper!"; and in Mexico, "Pim! Pum! Pam!." *Snap! Crackle! Pop!* own the double distinction of being both the first and the longest-lasting cartoon characters to represent a Kellogg product.

In 1928, *Kellogg's Rice Krispies* cereal entered the ready-to-eat cereal market. The company's advertising agency at that time, N. W. Ayer, was quick to capitalize on the toasted rice bubbles' most distinctive feature - they make noise in milk. This made *Rice Krispies®* cereal the perfect product to sponsor Kellogg Company's first venture into national radio - a popular children's story program called "The Singing Lady," produced in Chicago. The words they chose to describe this new cereal, "so crisp, it crackles in cream," were *Snap! Crackle! Pop!*.

These words without characters, first appeared on a *Rice Krispies* cereal package front in 1932. In 1933, a tiny gnome wearing a baker's hat and carrying a spoon topped a side panel. This gave *Snap!*, who always wears a baker's hat, some seniority. He still appeared solo on the packages as late as 1936, but *Crackle!* and *Pop!* joined him in print ads in the early '30s. By 1939, they starred in movie shorts. And finally, by the 1940s, they were together on side and back panels of packages sometimes as heroes of comic strips. During World War II, they patriotically posed with guns, tanks, and ships in ads that urged consumers to "Save time, save fuel, save energy."

According to one agency legend, the three gnomes didn't have their names until a creative layout artist extended lines from the cereal bowl so that the words *Snap! Crackle!* and *Pop!* landed on their hats - where they've been ever since.

In 1949, *Snap! Crackle!* and *Pop!* changed drastically from gnomes with huge noses and ears and oversized hats, to more human creatures with boyish haircuts, proportional features, and smaller hats. They continued to evolve as fashions changed, appearing with longer or shorter hair, rounder eyes, and different costumes. Their hats have changed least. *Snap!* always wears a baker's hat; *Crackle!*, a red or striped stocking cap; and *Pop!*, a military hat. From high-pitched elfin squeaks, their voices have developed more pleasant speaking and singing ranges. Since their television debut in the 1960s, they have become more animated.

Together, they've appeared in hundreds of ads and commercials and modeled for dozens of premiums. They love to sing and have performed several jingles. Their most popular song, written in 1963 by Dick Marx and Nick Winkless, is a mind-sticking three-part round called "Snap! Crackle! Pop! Rice Krispies." Kellogg used the jingle for four years. It still surfaces occasionally in nostalgic medleys and, according to one nightclub act, draws instant applause.

After 60 years in the business, SNAP! CRACKLE! and POP! are busier and more popular than ever, and they'll continue to ... their cereals make noise in milk.

90-622-004

Lazlo Toth
P.O. Box 245
Fairfax, California
94930 U.S.A.

TO: Vice President Dan Quale
From: Lazlo Toth

11 April 1992

RE: Values, Sacrifice, and Indiana

As an Official Member of the BUSH 92 QUALE Reelection Committee in California, I would like to offer some advice and ask a big favor.

Personally, I have no objection to you charging the cost of personal golf trips to the government. The newspapers say one of the trips cost taxpayers more than $10,000. That sounds like a lot, but on a per hole basis (18), it comes to less than $500 a hole, and divided by 200 million citizens, that golf trip cost a family of five less than a penny! Compared to the cost of a Scud missle or the daily interest on the deficit, it's like a peanut in the ballpark, but still, it's stories like this that get people upset.

President Bush has enough problems with the press tailgating him about his involvement in the S&L scandal, his "Official Residence" - a Houston hotel room, his role in the theft of Sitting Bull's scull, and his avoiding paying almost any state and local income tax, without worying about you flying off in military jets to fancy "Masons Only" country clubs, or having a special unit of White House marines on call to clean your cleats.

Frankly, the problem we face in November is not your being Vice President. But, if something should happen to President Bush, you would be President. That's the problem! That's what worries people! And President Bush's judgment about who he chooses to lead the nation in this unlikely event may become the main issue of the campaign - if he chooses you again. People feel as though we've been driving around with a flat for a spare. We've been lucky we haven't needed it, but a wise driver doesn't push his luck. He replaces his spare. Are you with me so far?

I know you and I share the goal of a second term for President Bush. So I ask you, on behalf of the Bush 92 Quale reelection committee, and The Fr. Junipero Serra Prayer Group, - For the good of America, for the flag we love, for the fifty states and Puerto Rico and Guam - do President Bush a favor, - please resign! Spare him from making the mistake of choosing you again! Step aside with honor! You can do it! Bravo Quale! Congradulations!

The state of Indiana needs you back in the Senate! Don't let them down!

Lazlo Toth

Lazlo Toth

Lazlo Toth
P.O. Box 245
Fairfax, California
94930 U.S.A.

President Richard M. Nixon   April 15, 1992
The Richard Nixon Library and Birthplace
Yorba Linda, California U.S.A. 9 2 6 8 6

Dear President Nixon,

   I was going through my attic recently and I ran across a bunch of letters
I received from you during those stormy days of "W". I won't mention the
word, you know what I mean. I was thinking maybe you'd like those letters
for your Library. It would show how you handled correspondence during
those difficult days of you-know-what-gate. So, if you're willing to frame
and display them at the L&B, I'll send them to you.
<u>One Request:</u> Could you check with your tax advisers to see if I can write
off the donated letters? Also, if you're a non profit organization, I need to
know if the Birthplace-Birdhouse you sold me is tax deductable? Can I write
off the whole $45 in one year, or does a purchase like that have to be
amortized? Let me know as soon as possible, I'm applying for an extension.

   Mr. President, Matter #2: Yesterday, I picked up my Elvis ballot at the
post office. But instead of going along with the flock and being railroaded
into voting for "A.- Young Elvis", or "B.- Old Elvis", I got the idea for a stamp
of Elvis in his prime. I took the liberty and used the photo I bought from
you ($5.50), to design a stamp I call "C.- Middle Elvis".
   If there's still time to get it on the ballot, considering the current voter
preference for "outsiders", I think it has a very good chance of winning.
   Mr. President!, I am mailing this entry to the Post Master General first
thing tomorrow. Soon, America will have one more chance to <u>Vote for Nixon!</u>

THE PRESIDENT AND THE KING AT THE WHITE HOUSE.

STAND BY OUR FLAG!

Lazlo Toth

Hair Club for Men, Ltd.
166 Geary Street (9th floor)
San Francisco, CA 94108

A HOLIDAY WISH FOR YOU.

Lazlo Toth
PO Box 245
Fairfax, CA 94

PLEASE
PLACE THIS
CARD IN
YOUR WALLET
IMMEDIATELY

YOUR
BE MA
YOUR NA
FROM OU

NORTH AMERICAN HUNTING CLUB

Look at these big benefits you get wi
American Hunting Club Official Memb
• Your own magazine, North American Hu
• New equipment field testing privileges.
• Keeping Track, members-only newsletter.
• Eligibility to win free hunting trips.
• Access to Outfitter/Guide Rating Service.
• Free Swap Hunt opportunities.
• Free gun give-aways to lucky members.
• Special members-only products and discounts.
• Your photo and story published in Club magazine.
• Membership kit and jacket patch.
...and that's not all!

Lazlo Toth
P.O. Box 24
Fairfax, CA   94930-0

52008406

H91F4

...if you return the winning number

FAIRFAX, CA RESIDD
...LAZLO TOTH...
HAS WON A GUARANTEE
TEN MILLION DOLLARS!

Ed McMahon of
NBC's Tonight Show

Dear Lazlo

Great ne
CALIFORNIA

We pa
you. LAZ

Are
milliona
paymen

If

R PRIZE winner has arrived at Yo

nd YOU.
e numbers

About the Author

Lurking not far behind the typewriter
of the mysterious crusader and super-
patriot, Lazlo Toth, is his prayer partner
and spelling consultant of twenty years,
Don Novello.

Novello is also known as Father Guido
Sarducci, the gossip columnist for
L'Osservatore Romano, the Vatican newspaper.

Originally from Ohio, he presently lives in
northern California.

multi-
with prize

OFFICIAL RULES—N

PUBLISHERS

ssing TEN MI

A, CA

FEB.14
GUARANTEED

URGENT:
Affix this seal
to enclosed
Entry-Order Card
and MAIL AT ONCE!

the residence of
LAZLO TOTH!
Therefore, if you return the winning number
time, it will be announced that --

LAZLO TOTH
IS THE MISSING
TEN MILLION DOLLAR W

This Is To Certify That American Family Publishers has posted financial
guarantees to assure payment of all prizes in these Sweepstakes,
including the TEN MILLION DOLLAR PRIZE that will be designa
payment to LAZLO TOTH of FAIRFAX, CALIFORNIA if the
the grand prize winning number by February 14